The Interpretation of the Bible in the Church

Edited by J. L. Houlden

SCM PRESS LTD

0 334 02589 3

First published 1995
by SCM Press Ltd,
26–30 Tottenham Road, London N1 4BZ

Typeset at The Spartan Press Ltd, Lymington, Hants
and printed in Great Britain by
Biddles Ltd, Guildford and King's Lynn

Contents

Preface

From a wider Christian perspective, *The Interpretation of the Bible in the Church*, produced by the Pontifical Biblical Commission in 1993, is perhaps the most remarkable and encouraging document to come from authorities within the Roman Catholic Church since the Second Vatican Council, or indeed ever. For good or ill, it strikes a positive yet discriminating note about those modern methods of biblical study which prevail in most of the mainstream churches (though often with some ambiguity) and in the academy. In the process, it provides a readable and all-round survey of those methods and their implications and drawbacks. This document is therefore significant not only for the Roman Catholic Church itself but also ecumenically and intellectually.

Issued as an official document, it has not so far been widely accessible, and the primary aim of this present volume is to remedy that defect. The hope is that it will receive the circulation and discussion that it surely deserves.

To assist that process and to add spice to it, the document is here accompanied by a number of articles giving various responses which it has elicited. The purpose is not to provide comprehensive treatment of the issues that the document raises, but to place it in context and to offer reasoned comment.

The articles are of two kinds. Some are pieces that have appeared in various papers and journals, representing a number of different points of view – Catholic, Anglican, Protestant, Jewish – and originating in a number of different places – the United Kingdom, the United States and Holland. These were in fact the only reviews that a fairly serious search managed to uncover – and that justified further the aim of the volume, to make the document more widely known.

Three of the articles have been specially commissioned, with a view to focussing on certain areas in which the document has apparent implications. Dr Muddiman writes out of his experience of formal Anglican-Roman Catholic dialogue and as a New Testament scholar. More critical of the document itself, Professor Carroll writes as a biblical scholar who is outside the churches and is deeply concerned that justice and truth should prevail where the biblical documents are concerned. Dr Stevenson's angle is the more oblique one of the liturgist, interested in what is after all much the most commonly experienced public appearance of scripture, the worship of the churches. There is, inevitably, some overlap, especially among the first class of articles, in the provision of basic explanatory material about the document.

In preparing this volume, I have been encouraged and helped at every stage by John Bowden of the SCM Press, who has done so much to further the ecumenical and academic causes to which we trust it will make a contribution.

I also wish to thank Linda Foster of the Press who has done the hard work on this book.

December 1994   Leslie Houlden

This book is offered in memory of Peter Hebblethwaite who died in December 1994. No one of his generation observed more acutely or interpreted more intelligently the activities and policies of the Vatican. He warmly encouraged the compilation of this book and is the author of the first response in Part Two.

Acknowledgments

Thanks are due to Libreria Editrice Vaticana for permission to reproduce the full authorized text of the Pontifical Biblical Commission's document; also to the Editor of *The Tablet* and to the late Peter Hebblethwaite for permission to reprint a slightly revised version of the latter's article; to the Editor of *The Church Times* for permission to reprint the article by Leslie Houlden; to the Editor of *First Things* for permission to reprint the articles by Paul M. Blowers, Jon D. Levenson and Robert L. Wilken; and to the Editor of *De Bazuin* for permission to reprint the article by Jan Holman.

PART ONE

THE INTERPRETATION OF THE BIBLE IN THE CHURCH

A Document from the Pontifical Biblical Commission

Preface

The study of the Bible is, as it were, the soul of theology, as the Second Vatican Council says, borrowing a phrase from Pope Leo XIII (*Dei Verbum*, 24). This study is never finished; each age must in its own way newly seek to understand the sacred books.

In the history of interpretation the rise of the historical-critical method opened a new era. With it, new possibilities for understanding the biblical word in its originality opened up. Just as with all human endeavour, though, so also this method contained hidden dangers along with its positive possibilities: The search for the original can lead to putting the word back into the past completely so that it is no longer taken in its actuality. It can result that only the human dimension of the word appears as real, while the genuine author, God, is removed from the reach of a method which was established for understanding human reality.

The application of a 'profane' method to the Bible necessarily led to discussion. Everything that helps us better to understand the truth and to appropriate its representations is helpful and worthwhile for theology. It is in this sense that we must seek how to use this method in theological research. Everything that shrinks our horizon and hinders us from seeing and hearing beyond that which is merely human must be opened up. Thus the emergence of the historical-critical method set in motion at the same time a struggle over its scope and its proper configuration which is by no means finished as yet.

In this struggle the teaching office of the Catholic Church has taken up positions several times. First, Pope Leo XIII, in his encyclical *Providentissimus Deus* of 18 November 1893, plotted out some markers on the exegetical map. At a time when liberalism was extremely sure of itself and much too intrusively dogmatic, Leo XIII was forced to express himself in a rather critical way, even though he did not exclude that which was positive from the new possibilities. Fifty years later, however, because of the fertile work of great Catholic exegetes, Pope Pius XII, in his encyclical *Divino Afflante Spiritu* of 30 September 1943, was able to provide largely positive encouragement toward making the modern methods of understanding the Bible fruitful. The Constitution on Divine Revelation of the Second Vatican Council, *Dei Verbum*, of 18 November 1965, adopted all of this. It provided us with a synthesis, which substantially remains, between the lasting insights of patristic theology and the new methodological understanding of the moderns.

In the meantime, this methodological spectrum of exegetical work has broadened in a way which could not have been envisioned thirty years ago. New methods and new approaches have appeared, from structuralism to materialistic, psychoanalytic and liberation exegesis. On the other hand, there are also new attempts to recover patristic exegesis and to include renewed forms of a spiritual interpretation of scripture. Thus the Pontifical Biblical Commission took as its task an attempt to take the bearings of Catholic exegesis in the present situation one hundred years after *Providentissimus Deus* and fifty years after *Divino Afflante Spiritu*.

The Pontifical Biblical Commission, in its new form after the Second Vatican Council, it not an organ of the teaching office, but rather a commission of scholars who, in their scientific and ecclesial responsibility as believing exegetes, take positions on important problems of scriptural interpretation and know that for this task they enjoy the confidence of the teaching office. Thus the present document was established. It contains a well-grounded overview of the panorama of present-day methods and in this way offers to the inquirer an orientation to the possibilities and limits of these approaches.

Accordingly, the text of the document inquires into how the meaning of scripture might become known – this meaning in which the human word and God's word work together in the singularity of historical events and the eternity of the everlasting Word, which is contemporary in every age. The biblical word comes from a real past. It comes not only from the past, however, but at the same time from the eternity of God and it leads us into God's eternity, but again along the way through time, to which the past, the present and the future belong.

I believe that this document is very helpful for the important questions about the right way of understanding holy scripture and that it also helps us to go further. It takes up the paths of the encyclicals of 1893 and 1943 and advances them in a fruitful way. I would like to thank the members of the Biblical Commission for the patient and frequently laborious struggle in which this text grew little by little. I hope that the document will have a wide circulation so that it becomes a genuine contribution to the search for a deeper assimilation of the word of God in holy scripture.

Rome, on the feast of St Matthew   Cardinal Joseph Ratzinger
the Evangelist 1933

Introduction

The interpretation of biblical texts continues in our own day to be a matter of lively interest and significant debate. In recent years the discussions involved have taken on some new dimensions. Granted the fundamental importance of the Bible for Christian faith, for the life of the church and for relations between Christians and the faithful of other religions, the Pontifical Biblical Commission has been asked to make a statement on this subject.

A. The state of the question today

The problem of the interpretation of the Bible is hardly a modern phenomenon, even if at times that is what some would have us believe. The Bible itself bears witness that its interpretation can be a difficult matter. Alongside texts that are perfectly clear, it contains passages of some obscurity. When reading certain prophecies of Jeremiah, Daniel pondered at length over their meaning (Daniel 9.2). According to the Acts of the Apostles, an Ethiopian of the first century found himself in the same situation with respect to a passage from the Book of Isaiah (Isaiah 53.7–8) and recognized that he had need of an interpreter (Acts 8.30–35). The Second Letter of Peter insists that 'no prophecy of scripture is a matter of private interpretation' (II Peter 1.20), and it also observes that the letters of the apostle Paul contain 'some difficult passages, the meaning of which the ignorant and untrained distort, as they do also in the case of the other scriptures, to their own ruin' (II Peter 3.16).

The problem is therefore quite old. But it has been accentuated with the passage of time. Readers today, in order to appropriate the words and deeds of which the Bible speaks, have to project themselves back almost twenty or thirty centuries – a process which always creates difficulty. Furthermore, because of the progress made in the human sciences questions of interpretation have become more complex in modern times. Scientific methods have been adopted for the study of the texts of the ancient world. To what extent can these methods be considered appropriate for the interpretation of holy scripture? For a long period the church in her pastoral prudence showed herself very reticent in responding to this question, for often the methods, despite their positive elements, have shown themselves to be wedded to positions hostile to the Christian faith. But a more positive attitude has also evolved, signalled by a whole series of pontifical documents, ranging from the encyclical *Providentissimus Deus* of Leo XIII (18 November 1893) to the encyclical *Divino Afflante Spiritu* of Pius XII (30 September 1943), and this has been confirmed by the declaration *Sancta Mater Ecclesia* of the Pontifical Biblical Commission (21 April 1964) and above all by the dogmatic constitution *Dei Verbum* of the Second Vatican Council (18 November 1965).

That this more constructive attitude has borne fruit cannot be denied. Biblical studies have made great progress in the Catholic Church, and the academic value of these studies has been acknowledged more and more in the scholarly world and among the faithful. This has greatly smoothed the path of ecumenical dialogue. The deepening of the Bible's influence upon theology has contributed to theological renewal. Interest in the Bible has grown among Catholics, with resultant progress in the Christian life. All those who have acquired a solid formation in this area consider it quite impossible to return to a pre-critical level of interpretation, a level which they now rightly judge to be quite inadequate.

But the fact is that at the very time when the most prevalent scientific method – the 'historical-critical method' – is freely practised in exegesis, including Catholic exegesis, it is itself brought into question. To some extent, this has come about in the scholarly world itself through the rise of alternative methods and approaches. But it has also arisen through the criticisms of many members of the faithful, who judge the method deficient from the point of view of faith. The historical-critical method, as its name suggests, is particularly attentive to the historical development of texts or traditions across the passage of time – that is, to all that is summed up in the term 'diachronic'. But at the present time in certain quarters it finds itself in competition with methods which insist upon a synchronic understanding of texts – that is, one which has to do with their language, composition, narrative structure and capacity for persuasion. Moreover, for many interpreters the diachronic concern to reconstruct the past has given way to a tendency to ask questions of texts by viewing them within a number of contemporary perspectives – philosophical, psychoanalytic, sociological, political, etc. Some value this plurality of methods and approaches as an indication of richness, but to others it gives the impression of much confusion.

Whether real or apparent, this confusion has brought fresh fuel to the arguments of those opposed to scientific exegesis. The diversity of interpretations only serves to show, they say, that nothing is gained by submitting biblical texts to the demands of scientific method; on the contrary, they allege, much is lost thereby. They insist that the result of scientific exegesis is only to provoke perplexity and doubt upon numerous points which hitherto had been accepted without difficulty. They add that it impels some exegetes to adopt positions contrary to the faith of the church on matters of great importance such as the virginal conception of Jesus and his miracles, and even his resurrection and divinity.

Even when it does not end up in such negative positions, scientific exegesis, they claim, is notable for its sterility in what concerns progress in the Christian life. Instead of making for easier and more secure access to the living sources of God's word, it makes of the Bible a closed book. Interpretation may always have been something of a problem, but now it requires such technical refinements as to render it a domain reserved for a few specialists alone. To the latter some apply the phrase of the Gospel: 'You have taken away the key of knowledge; you have not entered in yourselves and you have hindered those who sought to enter' (Luke 11.52; cf. Matthew 23.13).

As a result, in place of the patient toil of scientific exegesis, they think it necessary to substitute simpler approaches such as one or other of the various forms of synchronic reading which may be considered appropriate. Some even, turning their backs upon all

Pentecostal Approach

ᴬ study, advocate a so-called 'spiritual' reading of the Bible, by which they understand a reading guided solely by personal inspiration – one that is subjective – and intended only to nourish such inspiration. Some seek above all to find in the Bible the Christ of their own personal vision and, along with it, the satisfaction of their own spontaneous religious feelings. Others claim to find there immediate answers to all kinds of questions touching both their own lives and that of the community. There are, moreover, numerous sects which propose as the only way of interpretation one that has been revealed to them alone.

B. Purpose of this document

It is, then, appropriate to give serious consideration to the various aspects of the present situation as regards the interpretation of the Bible – to attend to the criticisms and the complaints as also to the hopes and aspirations which are being expressed in this matter, to assess the possibilities opened up by the new methods and approaches and, finally, to try to determine more precisely the direction which best corresponds to the mission of exegesis in the Catholic Church.

Such is the purpose of this document. The Pontifical Biblical Commission desires to indicate the paths most appropriate for arriving at an interpretation of the Bible as faithful as possible to its character both human and divine. The commission does not aim to adopt a position on all the questions which arise with respect to the Bible such as, for example, the theology of inspiration. What it has in mind is to examine all the methods likely to contribute effectively to the task of making more available the riches contained in the biblical texts. The aim is that the word of God may become more and more the spiritual nourishment of the members of the people of God, the source for them of a life of faith, of hope and of love – and indeed a light for all humanity (cf. *Dei Verbum*, 21).

To accomplish this goal, the present document:

1. Will give a brief description of the various methods and approaches, indicating the possibilities they offer and their

limitations. (By an exegetical *method*, we understand a group of scientific procedures employed in order to explain texts. We speak of an *approach* when it is a question of an inquiry proceeding from a particular point of view.)

2. Will examine certain questions of a hermeneutical nature.

3. Will reflect upon the aspects which may be considered characteristic of a Catholic interpretation of the Bible and upon its relationship with other theological disciplines.

4. Will consider, finally, the place interpretation of the Bible has in the life of the church.

I

Methods and Approaches for Interpretation

A. Historical-critical method

The historical-critical method is the indispensable method for the scientific study of the meaning of ancient texts. Holy scripture, inasmuch as it is the 'word of God in human language', has been composed by human authors in all its various parts and in all the sources that lie behind them. Because of this, its proper understanding not only admits the use of this method but actually requires it.

1. History of the method

For a correct understanding of this method as currently employed, a glance over its history will be of assistance. Certain elements of this method of interpretation are very ancient. They were used in antiquity by Greek commentators of classical literature and, much later, in the course of the patristic period by authors such as Origen, Jerome and Augustine. The method at that time was much less developed. Its modern forms are the result of refinements brought about especially since the time of the Renaissance humanists and their *recursus ad fontes* (return to the sources).

The textual criticism of the New Testament was able to be developed as a scientific discipline only from about 1800 onward, after its link with the *textus receptus* was severed. But the beginnings of literary criticism go back to the seventeenth century, to the work of Richard Simon, who drew attention to the doublets, discrepancies in content and differences of style observable in the Pentateuch – discoveries not easy to reconcile with the attribution of the entire text to Moses as single author. In the eighteenth century, Jean Astruc was still satisfied that the matter could be explained on the basis that Moses had made use of various sources (especially two principal ones) to compose the Book of Genesis. But as time passed biblical critics contested the Mosaic authorship of the Pentateuch with ever growing confidence.

Literary criticism for a long time came to be identified with the attempt to distinguish in texts different sources. Thus it was that there developed in the nineteenth century the 'documentary hypothesis', which sought to give an explanation of the editing of the Pentateuch. According to this hypothesis, four documents, to some extent parallel with each other, had been woven together: that of the Yahwist (J), that of the Elohist (E), that of the Deuteronomist (D) and that of the priestly author (P); the final editor made use of this latter (priestly) document to provide a structure for the whole.

In similar fashion, to explain both the agreements and disagreements between the three Synoptic Gospels, scholars had recourse to the 'two source' hypothesis. According to this, the Gospels of Matthew and Luke were composed out of two principal sources: on the one hand, the Gospel of Mark and, on the other, a collection of the sayings of Jesus (called *Q*, from the German word *Quelle*, meaning 'source'). In their essential features, these two hypotheses retain their prominence in scientific exegesis today – though they are also under challenge.

In the desire to establish the chronology of the biblical texts, this kind of literary criticism restricted itself to the task of dissecting and dismantling the text in order to identify the various sources. It did not pay sufficient attention to the final form of the biblical text and to the message which it conveyed in the state in which it actually exists (the contribution of editors was not held in high regard). This meant that historical-critical exegesis could often seem to be something which simply dissolved and destroyed the text. This was all the more the case when, under the influence of the comparative history of religions, such as it then was, or on the basis of certain philosophical ideas, some exegetes expressed highly negative judgments against the Bible.

It was Hermann Gunkel who brought the method out of the ghetto of literary criticism understood in this way. Although he continued to regard the books of the Pentateuch as compilations, he attended to the particular texture of the different elements of the text. He sought to define the genre of each piece (e.g., whether 'legend' or 'hymn') and its original setting in the life of the community or *Sitz im Leben* (e.g., a legal setting or a liturgical one, etc.).

To this kind of research into literary genres was joined the 'critical study of forms'· (*Formgeschichte*), which Martin Dibelius and Rudolf Bultmann introduced into the exegesis of the Synoptic Gospels. Bultmann combined form-critical studies with a biblical hermeneutic inspired by the existentialist philosophy of Martin Heidegger. As a result, *Formgeschichte* often stirred up serious reservations.

But one of the results of this method has been to demonstrate more clearly that the tradition recorded in the New Testament had its origin and found its basic shape within Christian community or early church, passing from the preaching of Jesus himself to that which proclaimed that Jesus is the Christ. Eventually, form criticism was supplemented by *Redaktionsgeschichte* (redaction criticism), the 'critical study of the process of editing'. This sought to shed light upon the personal contribution of each evangelist and to uncover the theological tendencies which shaped his editorial work.

When this last method was brought into play, the whole series of different stages chacteristic of the historical-critical method became complete: from textual criticism one progresses to literary criticism, with its work of dissection in the quest for sources; then one moves to a critical study of forms and, finally, to an analysis of the editorial process, which aims to be particularly attentive to the text as it has been put together. All this has made it possible to understand far more accurately the intention of the authors and editors of the Bible as well as the message which they addressed to their first readers. The achievement of these results has lent the historical-critical method an importance of the highest order.

2. Principles

The fundamental principles of the historical-critical method in its classic form are the following:

It is a historical method, not only because it is applied to ancient texts – in this case, those of the Bible – and studies their significance from a historical point of view, but also and above all because it seeks to shed light upon the historical processes which gave rise to biblical texts, diachronic processes that were often complex and involved a long period of time. At the different stages of their production, the texts of the Bible were addressed to various categories of hearers or readers living in different places and different times.

It is a critical method because in each of its steps (from textual criticism to redaction criticism) it operates with the help of scientific criteria that seek to be as objective as possible. In this way it aims to make accessible to the modern reader the meaning of biblical texts, often very difficult to comprehend.

As an analytical method, it studies the biblical text in the same fashion as it would study any other ancient text and comments upon it as an expression of human discourse. However, above all in the area of redaction criticism, it does allow the exegete to gain a better grasp of the content of divine revelation.

3. Description

At the present stage of its development, the historical-critical method moves through the following steps:

Textual criticism, as practised for a very long time, begins the series of scholarly operations. Basing itself on the testimony of the oldest and best manuscripts, as well as of papyri, certain ancient versions and patristic texts, textual-criticism seeks to establish, according to fixed rules, a biblical text as close as possible to the original.

The text is then submitted to a linguistic (morphology and syntax) and semantic analysis, using the knowledge derived from historical philology. It is the role of literary criticism to determine the beginning and end of textual units, large and small, and to establish the internal coherence of the text. The existence of doublets, of irreconcilable differences and of other indicators is a clue to the composite character of certain texts. These can then be divided into small units, the next step being to see whether these in turn can be assigned to different sources.

Genre criticism seeks to identify literary genres, the social milieu that gave rise to them, their particular features and the history of their development. Tradition criticism situates texts in the stream of tradition and attempts to describe the development of this tradition over the course of time. Finally, redaction criticism studies the modifications that these texts have undergone before being fixed in their final state; it also analyses this final stage, trying as far as possible to identify the tendencies particularly characteristic of this concluding process.

While the preceding steps have sought to explain the text by tracing its origin and development within a diachronic perspective, this last step concludes with a study that is synchronic. At this point the text is explained as it stands, on the basis of the mutual relationships between its diverse elements, and with an eye to its character as a message communicated by the author to his contemporaries. At this point one is in a position to consider the demands of the text from the point of view of action and life (*fonction pragmatique*).

When the texts studied belong to a historical literary genre or are related to events of history, historical criticism completes literary criticism so as to determine the historical significance of the text in the modern sense of this expression.

It is in this way that one accounts for the various stages that lie behind the biblical revelation in its concrete historical development.

4. *Evaluation*

What value should we accord to the historical-critical method, especially at this present stage of its development?

It is a method which, when used in an objective manner, implies of itself no *a priori*. If its use is accompanied by *a priori* principles, that is not something pertaining to the method itself, but to certain hermeneutical choices which govern the interpretation and can be tendentious.

Oriented in its origins toward source criticism and the history of religions, the method has managed to provide fresh access to the Bible. It has shown the Bible to be a collection of writings, which most often, especially in the case of the Old Testament, are not the creation of a single author, but which have had a long prehistory inextricably tied either to the history of Israel or to that of the early church. Previously, the Jewish or Christian interpretation of the Bible had no clear awareness of the concrete and diverse historical conditions in which the word of God took root among the people; of all this it had only a general and remote awareness.

The early confrontation between traditional exegesis and the scientific approach, which initially consciously separated itself from faith and at times even opposed it, was assuredly painful; later however it proved to be salutary: Once the method was freed from external prejudices, it led to a more precise understanding of the truth of sacred scripture (cf. *Dei Verbum*, 12). According to *Divino Afflante Spiritu*, the search for the literal sense of scripture is an essential task of exegesis and, in order to fulfil this task, it is necessary to determine the literary genre of texts (cf. *Enchiridion Biblicum*, 560), something which the historical-critical method helps to achieve.

To be sure, the classic use of the historical-critical method reveals its limitations. It restricts itself to a search for the meaning of the biblical text within the historical circumstances that gave rise to it and is not concerned with other possibilities of meaning which have been revealed at later stages of the biblical revelation and history of the church. Nonetheless, this method has contributed to the production of works of exegesis and of biblical theology which are of great value.

For a long time now scholars have ceased combining the method with a philosophical system. More recently, there has been a tendency among exegetes to move the method in the direction of a greater insistence upon the form of a text, with less attention paid to its content. But this tendency has been corrected through the application of a more diversified semantics (the semantics of words, phrases, text) and through the study of the demands of the text from the point of view of action and life (*aspect pragmatique*).

With respect to the inclusion in the method of a synchronic analysis of texts, we must recognize that we are dealing here with a legitimate operation, for it is the text in its final stage, rather than in its earlier editions, which is the expression of the word of God. But diachronic study remains indispensable for making known the historical dynamism which animates sacred scripture and for shedding light upon its rich complexity: For example, the covenant code (Exodus 21–23) reflects a political, social and religious situation of Israelite society different from that reflected in the other law codes preserved in Deuteronomy (chapters 12–26) and in Leviticus (the holiness code, chapters 17–26). We must take care not to replace the historicizing tendency, for which the older historical-critical exegesis is open to criticism, with the opposite excess, that of neglecting history in favour of an exegesis which would be exclusively synchronic.

To sum up, the goal of the historical-critical method is to determine, particularly in a diachronic manner, the meaning expressed by the biblical authors and editors. Along with other methods and approaches, the historical-critical method opens up to the modern reader a path to the meaning of the biblical text such as we have it today.

B. New methods of literary analysis

No scientific method for the study of the Bible is fully adequate to comprehend the biblical texts in all their richness. For all its overall validity, the historical-critical method cannot claim to be totally sufficient in this respect. It necessarily has to leave aside many aspects of the writings which it studies. It is not surprising, then, that at the present time other methods and approaches are proposed which serve to explore more profoundly other aspects worthy of attention.

In this Section B, we will present certain methods of literary analysis which have been developed recently. In the following sections (C, D, E), we will examine briefly different approaches, some of which relate to the study of the tradition, others to the 'human sciences', others still to particular situations of the present time. Finally (F), we will consider the fundamentalist reading of the Bible, a reading which does not accept any systematic approach to interpretation.

Taking advantage of the progress made in our day by linguistic and literary studies, biblical exegesis makes use more and more of new methods of literary analysis, in particular rhetorical analysis narrative analysis and semiotic analysis.

1. Rhetorical analysis

Rhetorical analysis in itself is not, in fact, a new method. What is new is the use of it in a systematic way for the interpretation of the Bible and also the start and development of a 'new rhetoric'.

Rhetoric is the art of composing discourse aimed at persuasion. The fact that all biblical texts are in some measure persuasive in character means that some knowledge of rhetoric should be part of the normal scholarly equipment of all exegetes. Rhetorical analysis must be carried out in a critical way, since scientific exegesis is an undertaking which necessarily submits itself to the demands of the critical mind.

A considerable number of recent studies in the biblical area have devoted considerable attention to the presence of rhetorical features in scripture. Three different approaches can be distinguished. The first is based upon classical Graeco-Roman rhetoric; the second devotes itself to semitic procedures of composition; the third takes its inspiration from more recent studies – namely from what is called the 'new rhetoric'.

Every situation of discourse involves the presence of three elements: the speaker (or author), the discourse (or text) and the audience (or the addressees). Classical rhetoric distinguished accordingly three factors which contribute to the quality of a discourse as an instrument of persuasion: the authority of the speaker, the force of the argument and the feelings aroused in the audience. The diversity of situation and of audience largely determines the way of speaking adopted. Classical rhetoric since Aristotle distinguishes three modes of public speaking: the judicial mode (adopted in a court of law); the deliberative mode (for the political assembly) and the demonstrative mode (for celebratory occasions).

Recognizing the immense influence of rhetoric in Hellenistic culture, a growing number of exegetes make use of treatises on classical rhetoric as an aid toward analysing certain aspects of biblical texts, especially those of the New Testament.

Other exegetes concentrate upon the characteristic features of the biblical literary tradition. Rooted in semitic culture, this displays a distinct preference for symmetrical compositions, through which one can detect relationships between different elements in the text. The study of the multiple forms of parallelism and other procedures characteristic of the semitic mode of composition allows for a better discernment of the literary structure of texts, which can only lead to a more adequate understanding of their message.

The new rhetoric adopts a more general point of view. It aims to be something more than a simple catalogue of stylistic figures, oratorical stratagems and various kinds of discourse. It investigates what makes a particular use of language effective and successful in the communication of conviction. It seeks to be 'realistic' in the sense of not wanting to limit itself to an analysis that is purely formal. It takes due account of the actual situation of debate or discussion. It studies style and composition as means of acting upon an audience. To this end, it benefits from contributions made of late in other areas of knowledge such as linguistics, semiotics, anthropology and sociology.

Applied to the Bible, the new rhetoric aims to penetrate to the very core of the language of revelation precisely as persuasive religious discourse and to measure the impact of such discourse in the social context of the communication thus begun.

Because of the enrichment it brings to the critical study of texts, such rhetorical analysis is worthy of high regard, above all in view of the greater depth achieved in more recent work. It makes up for a negligence of long standing and can lead to the rediscovery or clarification of original perspectives that had been lost or obscured.

The new rhetoric is surely right in its drawing attention to the capacity of language to persuade and convince. The Bible is not simply a statement of truths. It is a message that carries within itself a function of communication within a particular context, a message which carries with it a certain power of argument and a rhetorical strategy.

Rhetorical analysis does have, however, its limitations. When it remains simply on the level of description, its results often reflect a concern for style only. Basically synchronic in nature, it cannot claim to be an independent method which would be sufficient by itself. Its application to biblical texts raises several questions. Did the authors of these texts belong to the more educated levels of society? To what extent did they follow the rules of rhetoric in their work of composition? What kind of rhetoric is relevant for the analysis of any given text: Graeco-Roman or semitic? Is there sometimes the risk of attributing to certain biblical texts a rhetorical structure that is really too sophisticated? These questions – and there are others – ought not in any way cast doubt upon the use of this kind of analysis; they simply suggest that it is not something to which recourse ought be had without some measure of discernment.

2. *Narrative analysis*

Narrative exegesis offers a method of understanding and communicating the biblical message which corresponds to the form of story and personal testimony, something characteristic of holy scripture and, of course, a fundamental modality of communication between human persons. The Old Testament in fact presents a story of salvation, the powerful recital of which provides the substance of the profession of faith, liturgy and catechesis (cf. Psalms 78.3–4; Exodus 12.24–27; Deuteronomy 6.20–25, 26.5–11). For its own part, the proclamatioin of the Christian kerygma amounts in essentials to a sequence telling the story of the life, death and resurrection of Jesus Christ, events of which the Gospels offer us a detailed account. Catechesis itself also appears in narrative form (cf. I Corinthians 11.23–25).

With respect to the narrative approach, it helps to distinguish methods of analysis, on the one hand, and theological reflection, on the other.

Many analytic methods are in fact proposed today. Some start from the study of ancient models of narrative. Others base themselves upon present-day 'narratology' in one or other of its forms, in which case there can often be points of contact with semiotics. Particularly attentive to elements in the text which have to do with plot, characterization and the point of view taken by a narrator, narrative analysis studies how a text tells a story in such a way as to engage the reader in its 'narrative world' and the system of values contained therein.

Several methods introduce a distinction between *real author* and *implied author*, *real reader* and *implied reader*.

The *real author* is the person who actually composed the story. By *implied author* one means the image of the author which the text progressively creates in the course of the reading (with his or her own culture, character, inclinations, faith, etc.). The *real reader* is any person who has access to the text – from those who first read it or heard it read, right down to those who read or hear it today. By *implied reader* one means the reader which the text presupposes and in effect creates, the one who is capable of performing the mental and affective operations necessary for entering into the narrative world of the text and responding to it in the way envisaged by the real author through the instrumentality of the implied author.

A text will continue to have an influence in the degree to which real readers (e.g., ourselves in the late twentieth century) can identify with the implied reader. One of the major tasks of exegesis is to facilitate this process of identification.

Narrative analysis involves a new way of understanding how a text works. While the historical-critical method considers the text as a 'window' giving access to one or other period (not only to the situation which the story relates but also to that of the community for whom the story is told), narrative analysis insists that the text also functions as a 'mirror' in the sense that it projects a certain image – a 'narrative world' – which exercises an influence upon readers' perceptions in such a way as to bring them to adopt certain values rather than others.

Connected with this kind of study, primarily literary in character, is a certain mode of theological reflection as one considers the implications the 'story' (and also the 'witness') character of scripture has with respect to the consent of faith and as one derives from this a hermeneutic of a more practical and pastoral nature. There is here a reaction against the reduction of the inspired text to a series of theological theses, often formulated in non-scriptural categories and language. What is asked of narrative exegesis is that it rehabilitate in new historical contexts the modes of communicating and conveying meaning proper to the biblical account in order to open up more effectively its saving power. Narrative analysis insists upon the need both to tell the story of salvation (the 'informative' aspect) and to tell the story in view of salvation (the 'performative' aspect). The biblical account, in effect, whether explicitly or implicitly as the case may be, contains an existential appeal addressed to the reader.

The usefulness of narrative analysis for the exegesis of the Bible is clear. It is well suited to the narrative character which so many biblical texts display. It can facilitate the transition, often so difficult, from the meaning of the text in its historical context (the proper object of the historical-critical method) to its significance for the reader of today. On the other hand, the distinction between the real author and the implied author does tend to make problems of interpretation somewhat more complex.

When applied to texts of the Bible, narrative analysis cannot rest content with imposing upon them certain pre-established models. It must strive to adapt itself to their own proper character. The synchronic approach which it brings to texts needs to be supplemented by diachronic studies as well. It must, moreover, beware of a tendency that can arise to exclude any kind of doctrinal elaboration in the content of biblical narratives. In such a case it would find itself out of step with the biblical tradition itself, which practises precisely this kind of elaboration, and also with the tradition of the church, which has continued further along the same way. Finally, it is worth noting that the existential subjective effectiveness of the impact of the word of God in its narrative transmission cannot be considered to be in itself a sufficient indication that its full truth has been adequately grasped.

3. Semiotic analysis

Ranged among the methods identified as synchronic, those namely which concentrate on the study of the biblical text as it comes before the reader in its final state, is semiotic analysis. This has experienced a notable development in certain quarters over the last twenty years. Originally known by the more general term *structuralism*, this method can claim as forefather the Swiss linguist Ferdinand de Saussure, who at the beginning of the present century worked out the theory according to which all language is a system of relationships obeying fixed laws. Several linguists and literary critics have had a notable influence in the development of the method. The majority of biblical scholars who make use of semiotics in the study of the Bible take as their authority Algirdas J. Greimas and the School of Paris, which he founded. Similar approaches and methods, based upon modern linguistics, have developed elsewhere. But it is Greimas-method which we intend to present and analyse briefly here.

Semiotics is based upon three main principles or presuppositions:

The principle of immanance: each text forms a unit of meaning complete in itself; the analysis considers the entire text but only the text; it does not look to any date 'external' to the text such as the author, the audience, any events it describes or what might have been its process of composition.

The principle of the structure of meaning: There is no meaning given except in and through relationship, in particular the relationship of 'difference'; the analysis of the text consists then in establishing the network of relationships (of opposition, confirmation, etc.) between the various elements; out of this the meaning of the text is constructed.

The principle of the grammar of the text: Each text follows a 'grammar', that is to say, a certain number of rules or structures; in the collection of sentences that we call discourse there are various levels, each of which has its own distinct grammar.

The overall content of a text can be analysed at three different levels.

The narrative level: Here one studies in the story the transformations which move the action from the initial to the final state. Within the course of the narrative, the analysis seeks to retrace the different phases, logically bound to each other, which mark the transformation from one state to another. In each of these phases it establishes the relationships between the 'roles' played by the 'actants' which determine the various stages of development and bring about transformation.

The level of discourse: The analysis here consists of three operations: (*a*) the fixing and classification of figures, that is to say, the elements of meaning in a text (actors, times, places); (*b*) the tracking of the course of each figure in the text in order to determine just how the text uses each one; (*c*) inquiry into the thematic value of the figures. This last operation consists in discerning 'in the name of what' (= what value) the figures follow such a path in the text determined in this way.

The logico-semantic level: This is the so-called deep level. It is also the most abstract. It proceeds from the assumption that certain forms of logic and meaning underlie the narrative and discursive organization of all discourse. The analysis at this level consists in identifying the logic which governs the basic articulations of the narrative and figurative flow of a text. To achieve this, recourse is often had to an instrument called the 'semiotic square' (*carré sémiotique*), a figure which makes use of the relationships between two 'contrary' terms and two 'contradictory' terms (for example, black and white; white and not-white; black and not-black).

The exponents of the theory behind the semiotic method continue to produce new developments. Present research centres most particularly upon enunciation and intertextuality. Applied in the first instance to the narrative texts of scripture, to which it is most readily applicable, the use of the method has been more and more extended to other kinds of biblical discourse as well.

The description of semiotics that has been given and above all the formulation of its presuppositions should have already served to make clear the advantages and the limitations of this method. By directing greater attention to the fact that each biblical text is a coherent whole, obedient to a precise linguistic mechanic of operation, semiotics contributes to our understanding of the Bible as word of God expressed in human language.

Semiotics can be usefully employed in the study of the Bible only in so far as the method is separated from certain assumptions developed in structuralist philosophy, namely the refusal to accept individual personal identity within the text and extratextual reference beyond it. The Bible is a word that bears upon reality, a word which God has spoken in a historical context and which God addresses to us today through the mediation of human authors. The semiotic approach must be open to history: first of all to the history of those who play a part in the texts; then to that of the authors and readers. The great risk run by those who employ semiotic analysis is that of remaining at the level of a formal study of the content of texts, failing to draw out the message.

When it does not become lost in remote and complex language and when its principal elements are taught in simple terms, semiotic analysis can give Christians a taste for studying the biblical text and discovering certain of its dimensions, without their first having to acquire a great deal of instruction in historical matters relating to the production of the text and its socio-cultural world. It can thus prove useful in pastoral practice itself, providing a certain appropriation of scripture among those who are not specialized in the area.

C. Approaches based on tradition

The literary methods which we have just reviewed, although they differ from the historical-critical method in that they pay greater attention to the internal unity of the texts studied, remain nonetheless insufficient for the interpretation of the Bible because they consider each of its writings in isolation. But the Bible is not a compilation of texts unrelated to each other; rather, it is a gathering together of a whole array of witnesses from one great tradition. To be fully adequate to the object of its study, biblical exegesis must keep this truth firmly in mind. Such in fact is the perspective adopted by a number of approaches which are being developed at present.

1. Canonical approach

The 'canonical' approach, which originated in the United States some twenty years ago, proceeds from the perception that the historical-critical method experiences at times considerable difficulty in arriving, in its conclusions, at a truly theological level. It aims to carry out the theological task of interpretation more successfully by beginning from within an explicit framework of faith: the Bible as a whole.

To achieve this, it interprets each biblical text in the light of the canon of scriptures, that is to say, of the Bible as received as the norm of faith by a community of believers. It seeks to situate each text within the single plan of God, the goal being to arrive at a presentation of scripture truly valid for our time. The method does not claim to be a substitute for the historical-critical method; the hope is, rather, to complete it.

Two different points of view have been proposed:

Brevard S. Childs centres his interest on the final canonical form of the text (whether book or collection), the form accepted by the community as an authoritative expression of its faith and rule of life.

James A. Sanders, rather than looking to the final and fixed form of the text, devotes his attention to the 'canonical process' or progressive development of the scriptures which the believing community has accepted as a normative authority. The critical study of this process examines the way in which older traditions have been used again and again in new contexts before finally coming to constitute a whole that is at once stable and yet adaptable, coherent while holding together matter that is diverse – in short, a complete whole in which the faith community can find its identity. In the course of this process various hermeneutic procedures have been at work, and this continues to be the case even after the fixing of the canon. These procedures are often midrashic in nature, serving to make the biblical text relevant for a later time. They encourage a constant interaction between the community and the scriptures, calling for an interpretation which ever seeks to bring the tradition up to date.

The canonical approach rightly reacts against placing an exaggerated value upon what is supposed to be original and early, as if this alone were authentic. Inspired scripture is precisely scripture in that it has been recognized by the church as the rule of faith. Hence the significance, in this light, of both the final form in which each of the books of the Bible appears and of the complete whole which all together make up as canon. Each individual book only becomes biblical in the light of the canon as a whole.

It is the believing community that provides a truly adequate context for interpreting canonical texts. In this context faith and the Holy Spirit enrich exegesis; church authority, exercised as a service of the community, must see to it that this interpretation remains faithful to the great tradition which has produced the texts (cf. *Dei Verbum*, 10).

The canonical approach finds itself grappling with more than one problem when it seeks to define the 'canonical process'. At what point in time precisely does a text become canonical? It seems reasonable to describe it as such from the time that the community attributes to it a normative authority, even if this should be before it has reached its final, definitive form. One can speak of a 'canonical' hermeneutic once the repetition of the traditions, which comes about through the taking into account of new aspects of the situation (be they religious, cultural or theological), begins to preserve the identity of the message. But a question arises: Should the interpretive process which led to the formation of the canon be recognized as the guiding principle for the interpretation of scripture today?

On the other hand, the complex relationships that exist between the Jewish and Christian canons of scripture raise many problems of interpretation. The Christian church has received as 'Old Testament' the writings which had authority in the Hellenistic Jewish community, but some of these are either lacking in the Hebrew Bible or appear there in somewhat different form. The corpus is therefore different. From this it follows that the canonical interpretation cannot be identical in each case, granted that each text must be read in relation to the whole corpus. But, above all, the church reads the Old Testament in the light of the paschal mystery – the death and resurrection of Jesus Christ – who brings a radical newness and, with sovereign authority, gives a meaning to the scriptures that is decisive and definitive (cf. *Dei Verbum*, 4). This new determination of meaning has become an integral element of Christian faith. It ought not, however, mean doing away with all attempt to be consistent with that earlier canonical interpretation which preceded the Christian Passover. One must respect each stage of the history of salvation. To empty out of the Old Testament its own proper meaning would be to deprive the New of its roots in history.

2. *Approach through recourse to Jewish traditions of interpretation*

The Old Testament reached its final form in the Jewish world of the four or five centuries preceding the Christian era. Judaism of this time also provided the matrix for the origin of the New Testament and the infant church. Numerous studies of the history of ancient

Judaism and notably the manifold research stimulated by the discoveries at Qumran have highlighted the complexity of the Jewish world, both in the land of Israel and in the Diaspora, throughout this period.

It is in this world that the interpretation of scripture had its beginning. One of the most ancient witnesses to the Jewish interpretation of the Bible is the Greek translation known as the Septuagint. The Aramaic Targums represent a further witness to the same activity which has carried on down to the present, giving rise in the process to an immense mass of learned procedures for the preservation of the text of the Old Testament and for the explanation of the meaning of biblical texts. At all stages, the more astute Christian exegetes, from Origen and Jerome onward, have sought to draw profit from the Jewish biblical learning in order to acquire a better understanding of scripture. Many modern exegetes follow this example.

The ancient Jewish traditions allow for a better understanding particularly of the Septuagint, the Jewish Bible which eventually became the first part of the Christian Bible for at least the first four centuries of the church and has remained so in the East down to the present day. The extracanonical Jewish literature, called apocryphal or intertestamental, in its great abundance and variety, is an important source for the interpretation of the New Testament. The variety of exegetical procedures practiced by the different strains of Judaism can actually be found within the Old Testament itself, for example in Chronicles with reference to the books of Samuel and Kings, and also within the New Testament, as for example in certain ways Paul goes about argument from scripture. A great variety of forms – parables, allegories, anthologies and *florilegia*, rereadings (*relectures*), *pesher* technique, methods of associating otherwise unrelated texts, psalms and hymns, vision, revelation and dream sequences, wisdom compositions – all are common to both the Old and the New Testaments as well as in Jewish circles before and after the time of Jesus. The Targums and the Midrashic literature illustrate the homiletic tradition and mode of biblical interpretation practised by wide sectors of Judaism in the first centuries.

Many Christian exegetes of the Old Testament look besides to the Jewish commentators, grammarians and lexicographers of the mediaeval and more recent periods as a resource for understanding difficult passages or expressions that are either rare or unique. References to such Jewish works appear in current exegetical discussion much more frequently than was formerly the case.

Jewish biblical scholarship in all its richness, from its origins in antiquity down to the present day, is an asset of the highest value for the exegesis of both Testaments, provided that it be used with discretion. Ancient Judaism took many diverse forms. The Pharisaic form which eventually came to be the most prevalent, in the shape of rabbinic Judaism, was by no means the only one. The range of ancient Jewish texts extends across several centuries; it is important to rank them in chronological order before proceeding to make comparisons. Above all the overall pattern of the Jewish and Christian communities is very different. On the Jewish side, in very varied ways, it is a question of a religion which defines a people and a way of life based upon written revelation and an oral tradition; whereas, on the Christian side, it is faith in the Lord Jesus – the one who died, was raised and lives still, Messiah and Son of God; it is around faith in his person that the community is gathered. These two diverse starting points create, as regards the interpretation of the scriptures, two separate contexts, which for all their points of contact and similarity are in fact radically diverse.

3. Approach by the history of the influence of the text (Wirkungsgeschichte)

This approach rests upon two principles: (*a*) a text only becomes a literary work in so far as it encounters readers who give life to it by appropriating it to themselves; (*b*) this appropriation of the text, which can occur either on the individual or community level and can take shape in various spheres (literary, artistic, theological, ascetical and mystical), contributes to a better understanding of the text itself.

Without being entirely unknown in antiquity, this approach was developed in literary studies between 1960 and 1970, a time when criticism became interested in the relation between a text and its readers. Biblical studies can only draw profit from research of this kind, all the more so since the philosophy of hermeneutics for its own part stresses the necessary distance between a work and its author as well as between a work and its readers. Within this perspective, the history of the effect produced by a book or a passage of scripture (*Wirkungsgeschichte*) begins to enter into the work of interpretation. Such an inquiry seeks to assess the development of interpretation over the course of time under the influence of the concerns readers have brought to the text. It also attempts to evaluate the importance of the role played by tradition in finding meaning in biblical texts.

The mutual presence to each other of text and readers creates its own dynamic, for the text exercises an influence and provokes reactions. It makes a resonant claim that is heard by readers, whether as individuals or as members of a group. The reader is in any case never an isolated subject. He or she belongs to a social context and lives within a tradition. Readers come to the text with their own questions, exercise a certain selectivity, propose an interpretation and, in the end, are able to create a further work or else take initiatives inspired directly from their reading of scripture.

Numerous examples of such an approach are already evident. The history of the reading of the Song of Songs offers an excellent illustration: it would show how this book was received in the patristic period, in monastic circles of the mediaeval church and then again how it was taken up by a mystical writer such as St John of the Cross. The approach thus offers a better chance of uncovering all the dimensions of meaning contained in such a writing. Similarly, in the New Testament it is both possible and useful to throw light upon the meaning of a passage (for example, that of the rich young man in Matthew 19.16–26) by pointing out how fruitful its influence has been throughout the history of the church.

At the same time, history also illustrates the prevalence from time too time of interpretations that are tendentious and false, baneful in their effect – such as, for example, those that have promoted anti-semitism or other forms of racial discrimination or, yet again, various kinds of millenarian delusions. This serves to show that this approach cannot constitute a discipline that would be purely autonomous. Discernment is required. Care must be exercised not to privilege one or other stage of the history of the text's influence to such an extent that it becomes the sole norm of its interpretation for all time.

D. Approaches that use the human sciences

In order to communicate itself, the word of God has taken root in the life of human communities (cf. Sirach 24.12), and it has been through the psychological dispositions of the various persons who composed the biblical writings that it has pursued its path. It follows, then, that the human sciences – in particular, sociology, anthropology and psychology – can contribute toward a better understanding of certain aspects of biblical texts. It should be noted, however, that in this area there are several schools of thought, with notable disagreement among them on the very nature of these sciences. That said, a good number of exegetes have drawn considerable profit in recent years from research of this kind.

1. *Sociological approach*

Religious texts are bound in reciprocal relationship to the societies in which they originate. This is clearly the case as regards biblical texts. Consequently, the scientific study of the Bible requires as exact a knowledge as is possible of the social conditions distinctive of the various milieus in which the traditions recorded in the Bible took shape. This kind of socio-historical information needs then to be completed by an accurate sociological explanation, which will provide a scientific interpretation of the implications for each case of the prevailing social conditions.

The sociological point of view has had a role in the history of exegesis for quite some time. The attention which form criticism devoted to the social circumstances in which various texts arose (*Sitz im Leben*) is already an indication of this: It recognized that biblical traditions bore the mark of the socio-cultural milieu which transmitted them. In the first third of the twentieth century, the Chicago School studied the socio-historical situation of early Christianity, thereby giving historical criticism a notable impulse in this direction. In the course of the last twenty years (1970–1990), the sociological approach to biblical texts has become an integral part of exegesis.

The questions which arise in this area for the exegesis of the Old Testament are manifold. One should ask, for example, concerning the various forms of social and religious organization which Israel has known in the course of its history. For the period before the formation of a nation-state, does the ethnological model of a society which is segmentary and lacking a unifying head (*acephalous*) provide a satisfactory base from which to work? What has been the process whereby a loosely organized tribal league became, first of all, an organized monarchical state and, after that, a community held together simply by bonds of religion and common descent? What economic, military and other transformations were brought about by the movement toward political and religious centralization that led to the monarchy? Does not the study of the laws regulating social behaviour in the ancient Near East and in Israel make a more useful contribution to the understanding of the Decalogue than purely literary attempts to reconstruct the earliest form of the text?

For the exegesis of the New Testament, the questions will clearly be somewhat different. Let us mention some: to account for the way of life adopted by Jesus and his disciples before Easter, what value can be accorded to the theory of a movement of itinerant charismatic figures, living without fixed home, without family, without money and other goods? In the matter of the call to follow in the steps of Jesus, can we speak of a genuine relationship of continuity between the radical detachment involved in following Jesus in his earthly life and what was asked of members of the Christian movement after Easter in the very different social conditions of early Christianity? What do we know of the social structure of the Pauline communities, taking account in each case of the relevant urban culture?

In general, the sociological approach broadens the exegetical enterprise and brings to it many positive aspects. Knowledge of sociological data which help us understand the economic, cultural and religious functioning of the biblical world is indispensable for historical criticism. The task incumbent upon the exegete to gain a better understanding of the early church's witness to faith cannot be achieved in a fully rigorous way without the scientific research which studies the strict relationship that exists between the texts of the New Testament and life as actually lived by the early church. The employment of models provided by sociological science offers historical studies into the biblical period a notable potential for renewal – though it is necessary, of course, that the models employed be modified in accordance with the reality under study.

Here let us signal some of the risks involved in applying the sociological approach to exegesis. It is surely the case that, if the work of sociology consists in the study of currently existing societies, one can expect difficulty when seeking to apply its methods to historical societies belonging to a very distant past. Biblical and extrabiblical texts do not necessarily provide the sort of documentation adequate to give a comprehensive picture of the society of the time. Moreover, the sociological method does tend to pay rather more attention to the economic and institutional aspects of human life than to its personal and religious dimensions.

2. *The approach through cultural anthropology*

The approach to biblical texts which makes use of the study of cultural anthropology stands in close relationship with the sociological approach. The distinction between the two approaches exists, at one and the same time, on the level of perception, on that of method and on that of the aspect of reality under consideration. While the sociological approach – as we have just mentioned – studies economic and institutional aspects above all, the anthropological approach is interested in a wide assortment of other aspects, reflected in language, art, religion, but also in dress, ornament, celebration, dance, myth, legend and all that concerns ethnography.

In general, cultural anthropology seeks to define the characteristics of different kinds of human beings in their social context – as, for example, the 'Mediterranean person' – with all that this involves by way of studying the rural or urban context and with attention paid to the values recognized by the society in question (honour and dishonour, secrecy, of keeping faith, tradition, kinds of education and schooling), to the manner in which social control is exercised, to the ideas which people have of family, house, kin, to the situation of women, to institutionalized dualities (patron – client, owner – tenant; benefactor – beneficiary, free person – slave), taking into account also the prevailing conception of the sacred and the profane, taboos, rites of passage from one state to another, magic, the source of wealth, of power, of information, etc. On the basis of these diverse elements, typologies and 'models' are constructed, which are claimed to be common to a number of cultures.

Clearly this kind of study can be useful for the interpretation of biblical texts. It has been effectively applied to the study of the ideas of kinship in the Old Testament, of the position of women in Israelite society, of the influence of agrarian rituals, etc. In the texts which report the teaching of Jesus, for example the parables, many details can be explained thanks to this approach. This is also the case with regard to fundamental ideas, such as that of the reign of God or of the way of conceiving time with respect to the history of salvation, as well as of the processes by which the first Christians came to gather in communities. This approach allows one to distinguish more clearly those elements of the biblical message that are permanent, as having their foundation in human nature, and those which are more contingent, being due to the particular features of certain cultures. Nevertheless, no more than is the case with respect to other particularized approaches, this approach is not qualified simply by itself to determine what is specifically the content of revelation. It is important to keep this in mind when appreciating the valuable results it has brought.

3. Psychological and psychoanalytical approaches

Psychology and theology continue their mutual dialogue. The modern extension of psychological research to the study of the dynamic structures of the subsconscious has given rise to fresh attempts at interpreting ancient texts, including the Bible. Whole works have been devoted to the psychoanalytic interpretation of biblical texts, which has led to vigorous discussion: in what measure and under what conditions can psychological and psychoanalytical research contribute to a deeper understanding of sacred scripture?

Psychological and psychoanalytical studies do bring a certain enrichment to biblical exegesis in that, because of them, the texts of the Bible can be better understood in terms of experience of life and norms of behaviour. As is well known, religion is always in a relationship conflict or debate with the unconscious. It plays a significant role in the proper orientation of human drives. The stages through which historical criticism passes in its methodical study of texts need to be complemented by study of the different levels of reality they display. Psychology and psychoanalysis attempt to show the way in this respect. They lead to a multidimensional understanding of scripture and help decode the human language of revelation.

Psychology and, in a somewhat different way, psychoanalysis have led, in particular, to a new understanding of symbol. The language of symbol makes provision for the expression of areas of religious experience that are not accessible to purely conceptual reasoning but which have a genuine value for the expression of truth. For this reason, interdisciplinary study conducted in common by exegetes and psychologists or psychoanalysts offers particular advantages, especially when objectively grounded and confirmed by pastoral experience.

Numerous examples could be cited showing the necessity of a collaborative effort on the part of exegetes and psychologists: to ascertain the meaning of cultic ritual, of sacrifice, of bans, to explain the use of imagery in biblical language, the metaphorical significance of miracle stories, the wellsprings of apocalyptic visual and auditory experiences. It is not simply a matter of describing the symbolic language of the Bible but of grasping how it functions with respect to the revelation of mystery and the issuing of challenge – where the 'numinous' reality of God enters into contact with the human person.

The dialogue between exegesis and psychology or psychoanalysis, begun with a view to a better understanding of the Bible, should clearly be conducted in a critical manner, respecting the boundaries of each discipline. Whatever the circumstances, a psychology or psychoanalysis of an atheistic nature disqualifies itself from giving proper consideration to the data of faith. Useful as they may be to determine more exactly the extent of human responsibility, psychology and psychoanalysis should not serve to eliminate the reality of sin and of salvation. One should moreover take care not to confuse spontaneous religiosity and biblical revelation or impugn the historical character of the Bible's message, which bestows upon it the value of a unique event.

Let us note moreover that one cannot speak of 'psychoanalytical exegesis' as though it existed in one single form. In fact, proceeding from the different fields of psychology and from the various schools of thought, there exists a whole range of approaches capable of shedding helpful light upon the human and theological interpretation of the Bible. To absolutize one or other of the approaches taken by the various schools of psychology and psychoanalysis would not serve to make collaborative effort in this area more fruitful but rather render it harmful.

The human sciences are not confined to sociology, cultural anthropology and psychology. Other disciplines can also be very useful for the interpretation of the Bible. In all these areas it is necessary to take good account of competence in the particular field and to recognize that only rarely will one and the same person be fully qualified in both exegesis and one or other of the human sciences.

E. Contextual approaches

The interpretation of a text is always dependent on the mindset and concerns of its readers. Readers give privileged attention to certain aspects and, without even being aware of it, neglect others. Thus it is inevitable that some exegetes bring to their work points of view that are new and responsive to contemporary currents of thought which have not up till now been taken sufficiently into consideration. It is important that they do so with critical discernment. The movements in this regard which claim particular attention today are those of liberation theology and feminism.

1. The liberationist approach

The theology of liberation is a complex phenomenon, which ought not be oversimplified. It began to establish itself as a theological movement in the early 1970s. Over and beyond the economic, social and political circumstances of Latin America, its starting point is to be found in two great events in the recent life of the church: the Second Vatican Council, with its declared intention of *aggiornamento* and of orienting the pastoral work of the church toward the needs of the contemporary world, and the Second General Conference of the

Episcopate of Latin America held at Medellin in 1968, which applied the teachings of the council to the needs of Latin America. The movement has since spread also to other parts of the world (Africa, Asia, the black population of the United States).

It is not all that easy to discern if there truly exists 'one theology of liberation' and to define what its methodology might be. It is equally difficult to determine adequately its manner of reading the Bible, in a way which would lead to an accurate assessment of advantages and limitations. One can say that liberation theology adopts no particular methodology. But starting from its own socio-cultural and political point of view, it practices a reading of the Bible which is oriented to the needs of the people, who seek in the scriptures nourishment for their faith and their life.

Liberation theology is not content with an objectifying interpretation which concentrates on what the text said in its original context. It seeks a reading drawn from the situation of people as it is lived here and now. If a people lives in circumstances of oppression one must go to the Bible to find there nourishment capable of sustaining the people in its struggles and its hopes. The reality of the present time should not be ignored but, on the contrary, met head on, with a view to shedding upon it the light of the word. From this light will come authentic Christian praxis, leading to the transformation of society through works of justice and love. Within the vision of faith, scripture is transformed into a dynamic impulse for full liberation.

The main principles guiding this approach are the following:

God is present in the history of his people, bringing them salvation. He is the God of the poor and cannot tolerate oppression or injustice.

It follows that exegesis cannot be neutral, but must, in imitation of God, take sides on behalf of the poor and be engaged in the struggle to liberate the oppressed.

It is precisely participation in this struggle that allows those interpretations to surface which are discovered only when the biblical texts are read in a context of solidarity with the oppressed.

Because the liberation of the oppressed is a communal process, the community of the poor is the privileged addressee of the Bible as word of liberation. Moreover, since the biblical texts were written for communities, it is to communities in the first place that the reading

of the Bible has been entrusted. The word of God is fully relevant –
above all because of the capacity inherent in the 'foundational
events' (the exodus from Egypt, the passion and resurrection of
Jesus) – for finding fresh realization again and again in the course of
history.

Liberation theology includes elements of undoubted value: the
deep awareness of the presence of God who saves; the insistence on
the communal dimension of faith; the pressing sense of need for a
liberating praxis rooted in justice and love; a fresh reading of the
Bible which seeks to make of the word of God the light and the
nourishment of the people of God in the midst of its struggles and
hopes. In all these ways it underlines the capacity of the inspired text
to speak to the world of today.

But a reading of the Bible from a stance of such commitment also
involves some risks. Since liberation theology is tied to a movement
that is still in a process of development, the remarks which follow can
only be provisional.

This kind of reading is centred on narrative and prophetic texts
which highlight situations of oppression and which inspire a praxis
leading to social change. At times such a reading can be limited, not
giving enough attention to other texts of the Bible. It is true that
exegesis cannot be neutral, but it must also take care not to become
one sided. Moreover, social and political action is not the direct task
of the exegete.

In their desire to insert the biblical message into a socio-political
context, some theologians and exegetes have made use of various
instruments for the analysis of social reality. Within this perspective
certain streams of liberation theology have conducted an analysis
inspired by materialist doctrines, and it is within such frame of
reference that they have also read the Bible, a practice which is very
questionable, especially when it involves the Marxist principle of the
class struggle.

Under the pressure of enormous social problems, there has
understandably been more emphasis on an earthly eschatology.
Sometimes this has been to the detriment of the more transcendent
dimensions of scriptural eschatology.

More recent social and political changes have led this approach to
ask itself new questions and to seek new directions. For its further

development and fruitfulness within the church, a decisive factor will be the clarification of its hermeneutical presuppositions, its methods and its coherence with the faith and the tradition of the church as a whole.

2. *The feminist approach*

The feminist biblical hermeneutic had its origin in the United States toward the end of the nineteenth century. In the socio-cultural context of the struggle for the rights of women, the editorial board of a committee charged with the revision of the Bible produced *The Woman's Bible* in two volumes (New York 1885, 1898).

This movement took on fresh life in the 1970s and has since undergone an enormous development in connection with the movement for the liberation of women, especially in North America. To be precise, several forms of feminist biblical hermeneutics have to be distinguished, for the approaches taken are very diverse. All unite around a common theme: woman; and a common goal: the liberation of women and the acquisition on their part of rights equal to those enjoyed by men.

We can here mention three principal forms of feminist biblical hermeneutics: the radical form, the neo-orthodox form and the critical form.

The *radical* form denies all authority to the Bible, maintaining that it has been produced by men simply with a view to confirming man's age-old domination of woman (androcentrism).

The *neo-orthodox* form accepts the Bible as prophetic and as potentially of service, at least to the extent that it takes sides on behalf of the oppressed and thus also of women – this orientation is adopted as a 'canon within the canon' so as to highlight whatever in the Bible favours the liberation of women and the acquisition of their rights.

The *critical* form, employing a subtle methodology, seeks to rediscover the status and role of women disciples within the life of Jesus and in the Pauline churches. At this period, it maintains, a certain equality prevailed. But this equality has for the most part been concealed in the writings of the New Testament something which came to be more and more the case as a tendency toward patriarchy and androcentrism became increasingly dominant.

Feminist hermeneutic has not developed a new methodology. It employs the current methods of exegesis, especially the historical-critical method. But it does add two criteria of investigation.

The first is the feminist criterion, borrowed from the women's liberation movement, in line with the more general direction of liberation theology. This criterion involves a hermeneutic of suspicion: Since history was normally written by the victors, establishing the full truth requires that one does not simply trust texts as they stand but look for signs which may reveal something quite different.

The second criterion is sociological; it is based on the study of societies in the biblical times, their social stratification and the position they accorded to women. With respect to the New Testament documents, the goal of study, in a word, is not the idea of woman as expressed in the New Testament but the historical reconstruction of two different situations of woman in the first century: that which was the norm in Jewish and Graeco-Roman society and that which represented the innovation that took shape in the public life of Jesus and in the Pauline churches, where the disciples of Jesus formed 'a community of equals'. Galatians 3.28 is a text often cited in defence of this view. The aim is to rediscover for today the forgotten history of the role of women in the earliest stages of the church.

Feminist exegesis has brought many benefits. Women have played a more active part in exegetical research. They have succeeded, often better than men, in detecting the presence, the significance and the role of women in the Bible, in Christian origins and in the church. The world view of today, because of its greater attention to the dignity of women and to their role in society and in the church, ensures that new questions are put to the biblical text, which in turn occasions new discoveries. Feminine sensitivity helps to unmask and correct certain commonly accepted interpretations which were tendentious and sought to justify the male domination of women.

With regard to the Old Testament several studies have striven to come to a better understanding of the image of God. The God of the Bible is not a projection of a patriarchal mentality. He is Father, but also the God of tenderness and maternal love.

Feminist exegesis, to the extent that it proceeds from a preconceived judgment, runs the risk of interpreting the biblical texts in a tendentious and thus debatable manner. To establish its positions it must often, for want of something better, have recourse to arguments *e silentio*. As is well known, this type of argument is generally viewed with much reserve: It can never suffice to establish a conclusion on a solid basis. On the other hand, the attempt made on the basis of fleeting indications in the texts to reconstitute a historical situation which these same texts are considered to have been designed to hide – this does not correspond at all to the work of exegesis properly so called. It entails rejecting the content of the inspired texts in preference for a hypothetical construction, quite different in nature.

Feminist exegesis often raises questions of power within the church, questions which, as is obvious, are matters of discussion and even of confrontation. In this area, feminist exegesis can be useful to the church only to the degree that it does not fall into the very traps it denounces and that it does not lose sight of the evangelical teaching concerning power as service, a teaching addressed by Jesus to all disciples, men and women.[1]

F. Fundamentalist interpretation

Fundamentalist interpretation starts from the principle that the Bible, being the word of God, inspired and free from error, should be read and interpreted literally in all its details. But by 'literal interpretation' it understands a naively literalist interpretation, one, that is to say, which excludes every effort at understanding the Bible that takes account of its historical origins and development. It is opposed, therefore, to the use of the historical-critical method, as indeed to the use of any other scientific method for the interpretation of scripture.

The fundamentalist intepretation had its origin at the time of the Reformation, arising out of a concern for fidelity to the literal

[1] Out of nineteen votes cast, the text of this last paragraph received eleven in favour, four against and there were four abstentions. Those who voted against it asked that the result of the vote be published along with the text. The commission consented to this.

meaning of scripture. After the century of the Enlightenment it emerged in Protestantism as a bulwark against liberal exegesis.

The actual term *fundamentalist* is connected directly with the American Biblical Congress held at Niagara, NY in 1895. At this meeting, conservative Protestant exegetes defined 'five points of fundamentalism': the verbal inerrancy of scripture, the divinity of Christ, his virginal birth, the doctrine of vicarious expiation and the bodily resurrection at the time of the second coming of Christ. As the fundamentalist way of reading the Bible spread to other parts of the world, it gave rise to other ways of interpretation, equally 'literalist', in Europe, Asia, Africa and South America. As the twentieth century comes to an end, this kind of interpretation is winning more and more adherents, in religious groups and sects, as also among Catholics.

Fundamentalism is right to insist on the divine inspiration of the Bible, the inerrancy of the word of God and other biblical truths included in its five fundamental points. But its way of presenting these truths is rooted in an ideology which is not biblical, whatever the proponents of this approach might say. For it demands an unshakable adherence to rigid doctrinal points of view and imposes, as the only source of teaching for Christian life and salvation, a reading of the Bible which rejects all questioning and any kind of critical research.

The basic problem with fundamentalist interpretation of this kind is that, refusing to take into account the historical character of biblical revelation, it makes itself incapable of accepting the full truth of the incarnation itself. As regards relationships with God, fundamentalism seeks to escape any closeness of the divine and the human. It refuses to admit that the inspired word of God has been expressed in human language and that this word has been expressed, under divine inspiration, by human authors possessed of limited capacities and resources. For this reason, it tends to treat the biblical text as if it had been dictated word for word by the Spirit. It fails to recognize that the word of God has been formulated in language and expression conditioned by various periods. It pays no attention to the literary forms and to the human ways of thinking to be found in the biblical texts, many of which are the result of a process extending over long periods of time and bearing the mark of very diverse historical situations.

Fundamentalism also places undue stress upon the inerrancy of certain details in the biblical texts, especially in what concerns historical events or supposedly scientific truth. It often historicizes material which from the start never claimed to be historical. It considers historical everything that is reported or recounted with verbs in the past tense, failing to take the necessary account of the possibility of symbolic or figurative meaning.

Fundamentalism often shows a tendency to ignore or to deny the problems presented by the biblical text in its original Hebrew, Aramaic or Greek form. It is often narrowly bound to one fixed translation, whether old or present-day. By the same token it fails to take account of the 'rereadings' (*relectures*) of certain texts which are found within the Bible itself.

In what concerns the Gospels, fundamentalism does not take into account the development of the Gospel tradition, but naively confuses the final stage of this tradition (what the evangelists have written) with the initial (the words and deeds of the historical Jesus). At the same time fundamentalism neglects an important fact: The way in which the first Christian communities themselves understood the impact produced by Jesus of Nazareth and his message. But it is precisely there that we find a witness to the apostolic origin of the Christian faith and its direct expression. Fundamentalism thus misrepresents the call voiced by the gospel itself.

Fundamentalism likewise tends to adopt very narrow points of view. It accepts the literal reality of an ancient, out-of-date cosmology simply because it is found expressed in the Bible; this blocks any dialogue with a broader way of seeing the relationship between culture and faith. Its relying upon a non-critical reading of certain texts of the Bible serves to reinforce political ideas and social attitudes that are marked by prejudices – racism, for example – quite contrary to the Christian gospel.

Finally, in its attachment to the principle 'scripture alone', fundamentalism separates the interpretation of the Bible from the tradition, which, guided by the Spirit, has authentically developed in union with scripture in the heart of the community of faith. It fails to realize that the New Testament took form within the Christian church and that it is the holy scripture of this church, the existence of which preceded the composition of the texts. Because of this,

fundamentalism is often anti-church; it considers of little importance the creeds, the doctrines and liturgical practices which have
become part of church tradition, as well as the teaching function of
the church itself. It presents itself as a form of private interpretation
which does not acknowledge that the church is founded on the Bible
and draws its life and inspiration from scripture.

The fundamenalist approach is dangerous, for it is attractive to
people who look to the Bible for ready answers to the problems of
life. It can deceive these people, offering them interpretations that
are pious but illusory, instead of telling them that the Bible does not
necessarily contain an immediate answer to each and every problem.
Without saying as much in so many words, fundamentalism actually
invites people to a kind of intellectual suicide. It injects into life a
false certitude, for it unwittingly confuses the divine substance of the
biblical message with what are in fact its human limitations.

II

Hermeneutical Questions

A. Philosophical hermeneutics

In its recent course exegesis has been challenged to some rethinking in the light of contemporary philosophical hermeneutics, which has stressed the involvement of the knowing subject in human understanding, especially as regards historical knowledge. Hermeneutical reflection took new life with the publication of the works of Friedrich Schleiermacher, Wilhelm Dilthey and, above all, Martin Heidegger. In the footsteps of these philosophers, but also to some extent moving away from them, various authors have more deeply developed contemporary hermeneutical theory and its applications to scripture. Among them we will mention especially Rudolf Bultmann, Hans-Georg Gadamer and Paul Ricoeur. It is not possible to give a complete summary of their thought here. It will be enough to indicate certain central ideas of their philosophies which have had their impact on the interpretation of biblical texts. (The hermeneutic of the word developed by Gerhard Ebeling and Ernst Fuchs adopts a different approach and proceeds from another field of thought. It involves more a theological rather than a philosophical hermeneutic. Ebeling agrees, however, with such authors as Bultmann and Ricoeur in affirming that the word of God finds its true meaning only in the encounter with those to whom it is addressed.)

1. Modern perspectives

Conscious of the cultural distance between the world of the first century and that of the twentieth, Bultmann was particularly anxious to make the reality of which the Bible treats speak to his contemporaries. He insisted upon the 'pre-understanding' necessary for all understanding and elaborated the theory of the existential interpretation of the New Testament writings. Relying upon the thinking of Heidegger, Bultmann insisted that it is not possible to have an exegesis of a biblical text without presuppositions which guide comprehension. 'Pre-understanding' ('*Vorverständnis*') is founded upon the life-relationship ('*Lebensverhältnis*') of the interpreter to the reality of which the text speaks. To avoid subjectivism, however, one must allow pre-understanding to be deepened and enriched – even to be modified and corrected – by the reality of the text.

Bultmann asked what might be the most appropriate frame of thought for defining the sort of questions that would render the texts of scripture understandable to people of today. He claimed to have found the answer in the existential analysis of Heidegger, maintaining that Heideggerian existential principles have a universal application and offer structures and concepts most appropriate for the understanding of human existence as revealed in the New Testament message.

Gadamer likewise stresses the historical distance between the text and its interpreter. He takes up and develops the theory of the hermeneutical circle. Anticipations and preconceptions affecting our understanding stem from the tradition which carries us. This tradition consists in a mass of historical and cultural data which constitute our life context and our horizon of understanding. The interpreter is obliged to enter into dialogue with the reality at stake in the text. Understanding is reached in the fusion of the differing horizons of text and reader ('*Horizontverschmelzung*'). This is possible only to the extent that there is a 'belonging' ('*Zugehörigkeit*'), that is, a fundamental affinity between the interpreter and his or her object. Hermeneutics is a dialectical process: The understanding of a text always entails an enhanced understanding of oneself.

With regard to the hermeneutical thought of Ricoeur, the principal thing to note is the highlighting of the function of distantiation. This is the necessary prelude to any correct appropriation of a text. A first distancing occurs between the text and its author, for, once produced, the text takes on a certain autonomy in relation to its author; it begins its own career of meaning. Another distancing exists between the text and its successive readers; these have to respect the world of the text in its otherness.

Thus the methods of literary and historical analysis are necessary for interpretation. Yet the meaning of a text can be fully grasped only as it is actualized in the lives of readers who appropriate it. Beginning with their situation, they are summoned to uncover new meanings, along the fundamental line of meaning indicated by the text. Biblical knowledge should not stop short at language; it must seek to arrive at the reality of which the language speaks. The religious language of the Bible is a symbolic language which 'gives rise to thought' ('*donne à penser*'), a language the full richness of which one never ceases to discover, a language which points to a transcendent reality and which, at the same time, awakens human beings to the deepest dimensions of personal existence.

2. *Usefulness for exegesis*

What is to be said about these contemporary theories of the interpretation of texts? The Bible is the word of God for all succeeding ages. Hence the absolute necessity of a hermeneutical theory which allows for the incorporation of the methods of literary and historical criticism within a broader model of interpretation. It is a question of overcoming the distance between the time of the authors and first addressees of the biblical texts, and our own contemporary age, and of doing so in a way that permits a correct actualization of the scriptural message so that the Christian life of faith may find nourishment. All exegesis of texts is thus summoned to make itself fully complete through a 'hermeneutics' understood in this modern sense.

The Bible itself and the history of its interpretation point to the need for a hermeneutics – for an interpretation, that is, that proceeds from and addresses our world today. The whole complex of the Old and New Testament writings show themselves to be the product of a long process where founding events constantly find reinterpretation through connection with the life of communities of faith. In church tradition, the fathers, as first interpreters of scripture, considered that their exegesis of texts was complete only when it had found a meaning relevant to the situation of Christians in their own day. Exegesis is truly faithful to proper intention of biblical texts when it goes not only to the heart of their formulation to find the reality of faith there expressed but also seeks to link this reality to the experience of faith in our present world.

Contemporary hermeneutics is a healthy reaction to historical positivism and to the temptation to apply to the study of the Bible the purely objective criteria used in the natural sciences. On the one hand, all events reported in the Bible are interpreted events. On the other, all exegesis of the accounts of these events necessarily involves the exegete's own subjectivity. Access to a proper understanding of biblical texts is only granted to the person who has an affinity with what the text is saying on the basis of life experience. The question which faces every exegete is this: which hermeneutical theory best enables a proper grasp of the profound reality of which scripture speaks and its meaningful expression for people today?

We must frankly accept that certain hermeneutical theories are inadequate for interpreting scripture. For example, Bultmann's existentialist interpretation tends to enclose the Christian message within the constraints of a particular philosophy. Moreover, by virtue of the presuppositions insisted upon in this hermeneutic, the religious message of the Bible is for the most part emptied of its objective reality (by means of an excessive 'demythologization') and tends to be reduced to an anthropological message only. Philosophy becomes the norm of interpretation, rather than an instrument for understanding the central object of all interpretation: the person of Jesus Christ and the saving events accomplished in human history. An authentic interpretation of scripture, then, involves in the first place a welcoming of the meaning that is given in the events and, in a supreme way, in the person of Jesus Christ.

This meaning is expressed in the text. To avoid, then, purely subjective readings, an interpretation valid for contemporary times will be founded on the study of the text, and such an interpretation will constantly submit its presuppositions to verification by the text.

Biblical hermeneutics, for all that it is a part of the general hermeneutics applying to every literary and historical text, constitutes at the same time a unique instance of general hermeneutics. Its specific characteristics stem from its object. The events of salvation and their accomplishment in the person of Jesus Christ give meaning to all human history. New interpretations in the course of time can only be the unveiling or unfolding of this wealth of meaning.

Reason alone cannot fully comprehend the account of these events given in the Bible. Particular presuppositions, such as the faith lived in ecclesial community and the light of the Spirit, control its interpretation. As the reader matures in the life of the Spirit, so there grows also his or her capacity to understand the realities of which the Bible speaks.

B. The meaning of inspired scripture

The contribution made by modern philosophical hermeneutics and the recent development of literary theory allows biblical exegesis to deepen its understanding of the task before it, the complexity of which has become ever more evident. Ancient exegesis, which obviously could not take into account modern scientific require-ments, attributed to every text of scripture several levels of meaning. The most prevalent distinction was that between the literal sense and the spiritual sense. Mediaeval exegesis distinguished within the spiritual sense three different aspects, each relating, respectively, to the truth revealed, to the way of life commended and to the final goal to be achieved. From this came the famous couplet of Augustine of Denmark (thirteenth century):

> *Littera gesta docet, quid credas allegoria,*
> *moralis quid agas, quid speras anagogia.*

In reaction to this multiplicity of senses, historical-critical exegesis adopted, more or less overtly, the thesis of the one single meaning: a text cannot have at the same time more than one meaning. All the effort of historical-critical exegesis goes into defining 'the' precise sense of this or that biblical text seen within the circumstances in which it was produced.

But this thesis has now run aground on the conclusions of theories of language and of philosophical hermeneutics, both of which affirm that written texts are open to a plurality of meaning.

The problem is not simple, and it arises in different ways in regard to different types of texts: historical accounts, parables, oracular pronouncements, laws, proverbs, prayers, hymns, etc. Nevertheless, while keeping in mind that considerable diversity of opinion also prevails, some general principles can be stated.

1. The literal sense

It is not only legitimate, it is also absolutely necessary to seek to define the precise meaning of texts as produced by their authors – what is called the 'literal' meaning. St Thomas Aquinas had already affirmed the fundamental importance of this sense (*Summa Theologiae* I, q. 1, a. 10, ad 1).

The literal sense is not to be confused with the 'literalist' sense to which fundamentalists are attached. It is not sufficient to translate a text word for word in order to obtain its literal sense. We must understand the text according to the literary conventions of the time. When a text is metaphorical, its literal sense is not that which flows immediately from a word-to-word translation (e.g. 'Let your loins be girt': Luke 12.35), but that which corresponds to the metaphorical use of these terms ('Be ready for action'). When it is a question of a story, the literal sense does not necessarily imply belief that the facts recounted actually took place, for a story need not belong to the genre of history but be instead a work of imaginative fiction.

The literal sense of scripture is that which has been expressed directly by the inspired human authors. Since it is the fruit of inspiration, this sense is also intended by God, as principal author. One arrives at this sense by means of a careful analysis of the text, within its literary and historical context. The principal task of exegesis is to carry out this analysis, making use of all the resources of literary and historical research, with a view to defining the literal sense of the biblical texts with the greatest possible accuracy (cf. *Divino Afflante Spiritu: Ench. Bibl.* 550). To this end, the study of ancient literary genres is particularly necessary (ibid. 560).

Does a text have only one literal sense? In general, yes; but there is no question here of a hard and fast rule, and this for two reasons. First, a human author can intend to refer at one and the same time to more than one level of reality. This is in fact normally the case with regard to poetry. Biblical inspiration does not reject this capacity of human psychology and language; the Fourth Gospel offers numerous examples of it. Second, even when a human utterance appears to have only one meaning, divine inspiration can guide the expression in such a way as to create more than one meaning. This is the case with the saying of Caiaphas in John 11.50: At one and the same time it expresses both an immoral political ploy and a divine revelation. The two aspects belong, both of them, to the literal sense, for they are not made clear by the context. Although his example may be extreme, it remains significant, providing a warning against adopting too narrow a conception of the inspired text's literal sense.

One should be especially attentive to the dynamic aspect of many texts. The meaning of the royal psalms, for example, should not be limited strictly to the historical circumstances of their production. In speaking of the king, the psalmist evokes at one and the same time both the institution as it actually was and an idealized vision of kingship as God intended it to be; in this way the text carries the reader beyond the institution of kingship in its actual historical manifestation. Historical-critical exegesis has too often tended to limit the meaning of texts by tying it too rigidly to precise historical circumstances. It should seek rather to determine the direction of thought expressed by the text; this direction, far from working toward a limitation of meaning, will on the contrary dispose the exegete to perceive extensions of it that are more or less foreseeable in advance.

One branch of modern hermeneutics has stressed that human speech gains an altogether fresh status when put in writing. A written text has the capacity to be placed in new circumstances, which will illuminate it in different ways, adding new meanings to the original sense. This capacity of written texts is especially operative in the case of the biblical writings, recognized as the word of God. Indeed, what encouraged the believing community to preserve these texts was the conviction that they would continue to be bearers of light and life for generations of believers to come. The literal sense is, from the start, open to further developments, which are produced through the 'rereading' ('*relecture*') of texts in new contexts.

It does not follow from this that we can attribute to a biblical text whatever meaning we like, interpreting it in a wholly subjective way. On the contrary, one must reject as unauthentic every interpretation alien to the meaning expressed by the human authors in their written text. To admit the possibililty of such alien meanings would be equivalent to cutting off the biblical message from its root, which is the word of God in its historical communication; it would also mean opening the door to interpretations of a wildly subjective nature.

2. *The spiritual sense*

There are reasons, however, for not taking *alien* in so strict a sense as to exclude all possibility of higher fulfilment. The paschal event, the death and resurrection of Jesus, has established a radically new historical context, which sheds fresh light upon the ancient texts and causes them to undergo a change in meaning. In particular, certain texts which in ancient times had to be thought of as hyperbole (e.g. the oracle where God, speaking of a son of David, promised to establish his throne 'forever': II Samuel 7.12–13; I Chronicles 17.11–14), these texts must now be taken literally, because 'Christ, having been raised from the dead, dies no more' (Romans 6.9). Exegetes who have a narrow, 'historicist' idea about the literal sense will judge that here is an example of an interpretation alien to the original. Those who are open to the dynamic aspect of a text will recognize here a profound element of continuity as well as a move to a different level: Christ rules forever, but not on the earthly throne of David (cf. also Psalms 2.7–8; 110.1,4).

In such cases one speaks of 'the spiritual sense'. As a general rule we can define the spiritual sense, as understood by Christian faith, as the meaning expressed by the biblical texts when read, under the influence of the Holy Spirit, in the context of the paschal mystery of Christ and of the new life which flows from it. This context truly exists. In it the New Testament recognizes the fulfilment of the scriptures. It is therefore quite acceptable to reread the scriptures in the light of this new context, which is that of life in the Spirit.

The above definition allows us to draw some useful conclusions of a more precise nature concerning the relationship between the spiritual and literal senses:

Contrary to a current view, there is not necessarily a distinction between the two senses. When a biblical text relates directly to the paschal mystery of Christ or to the new life which results from it, its literal sense is already a spiritual sense. Such is regularly the case in the New Testament. It follows that it is most often in dealing with the

Old Testament that Christian exegesis speaks of the spiritual sense. But already in the Old Testament there are many instances where texts have a religious or spiritual sense as their literal sense. Christian faith recognizes in such cases an anticipatory relationship to the new life brought by Christy.

While there is a distinction between the two senses, the spiritual sense can never be stripped of its connection with the literal sense. The latter remains the indispensable foundation. Otherwise one could not speak of the 'fulfilment' of scripture. Indeed, in order that there be fulfilment, a relationship of continuity and of conformity is essential. But it is also necessary that there be transition to a higher level of reality.

The spiritual sense is not to be confused with subjective interpretations stemming from the imagination or intellectual speculation. The spiritual sense results from setting the text in relation to real facts which are not foreign to it: the paschal event, in all its inexhaustible richness, which constitutes the summit of the divine intervention in the history of Israel, to the benefit of all mankind.

Spiritual interpretation, whether in community or in private, will discover the authentic spiritual sense only to the extent that it is kept within these perspectives. One then holds together three levels of reality: the biblical text, the paschal mystery and the present circumstances of life in the Spirit.

Persuaded that the mystery of Christ offers the key to interpretation of all scripture, ancient exegesis laboured to find a spiritual sense in the minutest details of the biblical text – for example, in every prescription of the ritual law – making use of rabbinic methods or inspired by Hellenistic allegorical exegesis. Whatever its pastoral usefulness might have been in the past, modern exegesis cannot ascribe true interpretative value to this kind of procedure (cf. *Divino Afflante Spiritu: Ench. Bibl.* 553).

One of the possible aspects of the spiritual sense is the typological. This is usually said to belong not to scripture itself but to the realities expressed by scripture: Adam as the figure of Christ (cf. Romans 5.14), the flood as the figure of baptism (I Peter 3.20–21), etc. Actually, the connection involved in typology is ordinarily based on the way in which scripture describes the ancient reality (cf. the voice of Abel: Genesis 4.10; Hebrews 11.4; 12.24) and not simply on the reality itself. Consequently, in such a case one can speak of a meaning that is truly scriptural.

3. The fuller sense

The term *fuller sense* (*sensus plenior*), which is relatively recent, has given rise to discussion. The fuller sense is defined as a deeper meaning of the text, intended by God but not clearly expressed by the human author. Its existence in the biblical text comes to be known when one studies the text in the light of other biblical texts which utilize it or in its relationship with the internal development of revelation.

It is then a question either of the meaning that a subsequent biblical author attributes to an earlier biblical text, taking it up in a context which confers upon it a new literal sense, or else it is a question of the meaning that an authentic doctrinal tradition or a conciliar definition gives to a biblical text. For example, the context of Matthew 1.23 gives a fuller sense to the prophecy of Isaiah 7.14 in regard to the *almah* who will conceive, by using the translation of the Septuagint (*parthenos*): 'The *virgin* will conceive.' The patristic and conciliar teaching about the Trinity expresses the fuller sense of the teaching of the New Testament regarding God the Father, the Son and the Holy Spirit. The definition of original sin by the Council of Trent provided the fuller sense of Paul's teaching in Romans 5.12–21 about the consequences of the sin of Adam for humanity. But when this kind of control – by an explicit biblical text or by an authentic doctrinal tradition – is lacking, recourse to a claimed fuller sense could lead to subjective interpretations deprived of validity.

In a word, one might think of the 'fuller sense' as another way of indicating the spiritual sense of a biblical text in the case where the spiritual sense is distinct from the literal sense. It has its foundation in the fact that the Holy Spirit, principal author of the Bible, can guide human authors in the choice of expressions in such a way that the latter will express a truth the fullest depths of which the authors themselves do not perceive. This deeper truth will be more fully revealed in the course of time – on the one hand, through further divine interventions which clarify the meaning of texts and, on the other, through the insertion of texts into the canon of scripture. In these ways there is created a new context, which brings out fresh possibilities of meaning that had lain hidden in the original context.

III

Characteristics of Catholic
Interpretation

Catholic exegesis does not claim any particular scientific method as its own. It recognizes that one of the aspects of biblical texts is that they are the work of human authors, who employed both their own capacities for expression and the means which their age and social context put at their disposal. Consequently, Catholic exegesis freely makes use of the scientific methods and approaches which allow a better grasp of the meaning of texts in their linguistic, literary, socio-cultural, religious and historical contexts, while explaining them as well through studying their sources and attending to the personality of each author (cf. *Divino Afflante Spiritu: Ench. Bibl.* 557). Catholic exegesis actively contributes to the development of new methods and to the progress of research.

What characterizes Catholic exegesis is that it deliberately places itself within the living tradition of the church whose first concern is fidelity to the revelation attested by the Bible. Modern hermeneutics has made clear, as we have noted, the impossibility of interpreting a text without starting from a 'pre-understanding' of one type or another. Catholic exegetes approach the biblical text with a pre-understanding which holds closely together modern scientific culture and the religious tradition emanating from Israel and from the early Christian community. Their interpretation stands thereby in continuity with a dynamic pattern of interpretation that is found within the Bible itself and continues in the life of the church. This dynamic pattern corresponds to the requirement that there be a lived affinity between the interpreter and the object, an affinity which constitutes, in fact, one of the conditions that makes the entire exegetical enterprise possible.

All pre-understanding, however, brings dangers with it. As regards Catholic exegesis, the risk is that of attributing to biblical texts a meaning which they do not contain but which is the product of a later development within the tradition. The exegete must beware of such a danger.

A. Interpretation in the biblical tradition

The texts of the Bible are the expression of religious traditions which existed before them. The mode of their connection with these traditions is different in each case, with the creativity of the authors shown in various degrees. In the course of time, multiple traditions have flowed together little by little to form one great common tradition. The Bible is a privileged expression of this process: It has itself contributed to the process and continues to have controlling influence upon it.

The subject, 'interpretation in the biblical tradition', can be approached in very many ways. The expression can be taken to include the manner in which the Bible interprets fundamental human experiences or the particular events of the history of Israel, or again the manner in which the biblical texts make use of their sources, written or oral, some of which may well come from other religions or cultures – through a process of reinterpretation. But our subject is the interpretation of the Bible; we do not want to treat here these very broad questions but simply to make some observations about the interpretation of biblical texts that occurs within the Bible itself.

1. Rereadings (relectures)

One thing that gives the Bible an inner unity, unique of its kind, is the fact that later biblical writings often depend upon earlier ones. These more recent writings allude to older ones, create 'rereadings' (*relectures*) which develop new aspects of meaning, sometimes quite different from the original sense. A text may also make explicit reference to older passages, whether it is to deepen their meaning or to make known their fulfilment.

Thus it is that the inheritance of the land, promised by God to

Abraham for his offspring (Genesis 15.7, 18), becomes entrance into the sanctuary of God (Exodus 15.17), a participation in God's 'rest' (Psalms 132.7–8) reserved for those who truly have faith (Psalms 95.8–11; Hebrews 3.7–4.11) and, finally, entrance into the heavenly sanctuary (Hebrews 6.12, 18–20), 'the eternal inheritance' (Hebrews 9.15).

The prophecy of Nathan, which promised David a 'house', that is a dynastic succession, 'secure forever' (II Samuel 7.12–16), is recalled in a number of rephrasings (II Samuel 23.5; I Kings 2.4; 3.6; I Chronicles 17.11–14), arising especially out of times of distress (Psalms 89.20–38), not without significant changes; it is continued by other prophecies (Psalms 2.7–8; 110.1, 4; Amos 9.11; Isaiah 7.13–14; Jeremiah 23.36; etc.), some of which announce the return of the kingdom of David itself (Hosea 3.5; Jeremiah 30.9; Ezekiel 34.24; 37.24–25; cf. Mark 11.10). The promised kingdom becomes universal (Psalms 2.8; Daniel 2.35, 44; 7.14; cf. Matthew 28.18). It brings to fullness the vocation of human beings (Genesis 1.28; Psalms 8.6–9; Wisdom 9.2–3; 10.2).

The prophecy of Jeremiah concerning the seventy years of chastisement incurred by Jerusalem and Juda (Jeremiah 25.12; 29.10) is recalled in II Chronicles 25.20–23, which affirms that this punishment has actually occurred. Nonetheless, much later, the author of Daniel returns to reflect upon it once more, convinced that this word of God still conceals a hidden meaning that could throw light upon the situation of his own day (Daniel 9.24–27).

The basic affirmation of the retributive justice of God, rewarding the good and punishing the evil (Psalms 1.1–6; 112.1–10; Leviticus 26.3–33; etc.), flies in the face of much immediate experience, which often fails to bear it out. In the face of this, scripture allows strong voices of protestation and argument to be heard (Psalms 44; Job 10.1–7, 13.3–28, 23–24), as little by little it plumbs more profoundly the full depths of the mystery (Psalms 37; Job 38–42; Isaiah 53; Wisdom 3–5).

2. Relationships between the Old Testament and the New

Intertextual relationships become extremely dense in the writings of the New Testament, thoroughly imbued as it is with the Old

Testament through both multiple allusion and explicit citation. The authors of the New Testament accorded to the Old Testament the value of divine revelation. They proclaimed that this revelation found its fulfilment in the life, in the teaching and above all in the death and resurrection of Jesus, source of pardon and of everlasting life. 'Christ died for our sins according to the scriptures and was buried; he was raised on the third day according to the scriptures and appeared' (I Corinthians 15.3–5): Such is the centre and core of the apostolic preaching (I Corinthians 15.11).

As always, the relationship between scripture and the events which bring it to fulfilment is not one of simple material correspondence. On the contrary, there is mutual illumination and a progress that is dialectic: What becomes clear is that scripture reveals the meaning of events and that events reveal the meaning of scripture, that is, they require that certain aspects of the received interpretation be set aside and a new interpretation adopted.

Right from the start of his public ministry, Jesus adopted a personal and original stance different from the accepted interpretation of his age, that 'of the scribes and Pharisees' (Matthew 5.20). There is ample evidence of this: the antitheses of his Sermon on the Mount (Matthew 5.21–48); his sovereign freedom with respect to Sabbath observance (Mark 2.27–28 and parallels); his way of relativizing the precepts of ritual purity (Mark 7.1–23 and parallels); on the other hand, the radicality of his demand in other areas (Matthew 10.2–12 and parallels; 10.17–27 and parallels), and, above all, his attitude of welcome to 'the tax-collectors and sinners' (Mark 2.15–17 and parallels). All this was in no sense the result of a personal whim to challenge the established order. On the contrary, it represented a most profound fidelity to the will of God expressed in scripture (cf. Matthew 5.17; 9.13; Mark 7.8–13 and parallels; 10.5–9 and parallels).

Jesus' death and resurrection pushed to the very limit the interpretative development he had begun, provoking on certain points a complete break with the past, alongside unforeseen new openings. The death of the Messiah, 'king of the Jews' (Mark 15.26 and parallels), prompted a transformation of the purely earthly interpretation of the royal psalms and messianic prophecies. The resurrection and heavenly glorification of Jesus as Son of God lent these texts a fullness of meaning previously unimaginable. The result was that some expressions which had seemed to be hyperbole had now to be taken literally. They came to be seen as divine preparations to express the glory of Christ Jesus, for Jesus is truly 'Lord' (Psalms 110.1), in the fullest sense of the word (Acts 2.36; Philippians 2.10–11; Hebrews 1.10–12); he is Son of God (Psalms 2.7; Mark 14.62; Romans 1.3–4), God with God (Psalms 45.7; Hebrews 1.8; John 1.1; 20.28); 'his reign will have no end' (Luke 1.32–33; cf. I Chronicles 17.14; Psalms 45.7; Hebrews 1.8) and he is at the same time 'priest forever' (Psalms 110.4; Hebrews 5.6–10; 7.23–24).

It is in the light of the events of Easter that the authors of the New Testament read anew the scriptures of the Old. The Holy Spirit, sent by the glorified Christ (cf. John 15.26; 16.7), led them to discover the spiritual sense. While this meant that they came to stress more than ever the prophetic value of the Old Testament, it also had the effect of relativizing very considerably its value as a system of salvation. This second point of view which already appears in the Gospels (cf. Matthew 11.11–13 and parallels; 12.41–42 and parallels; John 4.12–14; 5.37; 6.32), emerges strongly in certain Pauline letters as well as in the Letter to the Hebrews. Paul and the author of the Letter to the Hebrews show that the Torah itself, in so far as it is revelation, announces its own proper end as a legal system (cf. Galatians 2.15–5.1; Romans 3.20–21; 6.14; Hebrews 7.11–19; 10.8–9). It follows that the pagans who adhere to faith in Christ need not be obliged to observe all the precepts of biblical law, from now on reduced in its entirety simply to the status of a legal code of a particular people. But in the Old Testament as the word of God they have to find the spiritual sustenance that will assist them to discover the full dimensions of the paschal mystery which now governs their lives (cf. Luke 24.25–27, 44–45; Romans 1.1–2).

All this serves to show that within the one Christian Bible the relationships that exist between the New and the Old Testament are quite complex. When it is a question of the use of particular texts, the authors of the New Testament naturally have recourse to the ideas and procedures for interpretation current in their time. To require them to conform to modern scientific methods would be anachronistic. Rather, it is for the exegete to acquire a knowledge of ancient techniques of exegesis so as to be able to interpret correctly the way in which a scriptural author has used them. On the other hand, it remains true that the exegete need not put absolute value in something which simply reflects limited human understanding.

Finally, it is worth adding that within the New Testament, as already within the Old, one can see the juxtaposing of different perspectives that sit sometimes in tension with one another: For example, regarding the status of Jesus (John 8.29, 16.32 and Mark 15.34) or the value of the Mosaic Law (Matthew 5.17–19 and Romans 6.14) or the necessity of works for justification (James 2.24 and Romans 3.28; Ephesians 2.8–9). One of the characteristics of the Bible is precisely the absence of a sense of systematization and the presence, on the contrary, of things held in dynamic tension. The Bible is a repository of many ways of interpreting the same events and reflecting upon the same problems. In itself it urges us to avoid excessive simplification and narrowness of spirit.

3. Some conclusions

From what has just been said one can conclude that the Bible contains numerous indications and suggestions relating to the art of interpretation. In fact, from its very inception the Bible has been itself a work of interpretation. Its texts were recognized by the communities of the former covenant and by those of the apostolic age as the genuine expression of the common faith. It is in accordance with the interpretative work of these communities and together with it that the texts were accepted as sacred scripture (thus, e.g. the Song of Songs was recognized as sacred scripture when applied to the relation between God and Israel). In the course of the Bible's formation, the writings of which it consists were in many cases reworked and reinterpreted so as to make them respond to new situations previously unknown.

The way in which sacred scripture reveals its own interpretation of texts suggests the following observations:

Sacred scripture has come into existence on the basis of a consensus in the believing communities recognizing in the texts the expression of revealed faith. This means that, for the living faith of the ecclesial communities, the interpretation of scripture should itself be a source of consensus on essential matters.

Granted that the expression of faith, such as it is found in the sacred scripture acknowledged by all, has had to renew itself continually in order to meet new situations, which explains the 're-readings' of many of the biblical texts, the interpretation of the Bible should likewise involve an aspect of creativity; it ought also to confront new questions so as to respond to them out of the Bible.

Granted that tensions can exist in the relationship between various texts of sacred scripture, interpretation must necessarily show a certain pluralism. No single interpretation can exhaust the meaning of the whole, which is a symphony of many voices. Thus the interpretation of one particular text has to avoid seeking to dominate at the expense of others.

Sacred scripture is in dialogue with communities of believers: it has come from their traditions of faith. Its texts have been developed in relation to these traditions and have contributed, reciprocally, to the development of the traditions. It follows that interpretation of scripture takes place in the heart of the church: in its plurality and its unity, and within its tradition of faith.

Faith traditions formed the living context for the literary activity of the authors of sacred scripture. Their insertion into this context also involved a sharing in both the liturgical and external life of the communities, in their intellectual world, in their culture and in the ups and downs of their shared history. In like manner, the interpretation of sacred scripture requires full participation on the part of exegetes in the life and faith of the believing community of their own time.

Dialogue with scripture in its entirety, which means dialogue with the understanding of the faith prevailing in earlier times, must be matched by a dialogue with the generation of today. Such dialogue will mean establishing a relationship of continuity. It will also involve acknowledging differences. Hence the interpretation of scripture involves a work of sifting and setting aside; it stands in continuity with earlier exegetical traditions, many elements of which it preserves and makes its own; but in other matters it will go its own way, seeking to make further progress.

B. Interpretation in the tradition of the church

The church, as the people of God, is aware that it is helped by the Holy Spirit in its understanding and interpretation of scripture. The first disciples of Jesus knew that they did not have the capacity right away to understand the full reality of what they had received in all its aspects. As they persevered in their life as a community, they experienced an ever-deepening and progressive clarification of the revelation they had received. They recognized in this the influence and the action of 'the Spirit of truth', which Christ had promised them, to guide them to the fullness of the truth (John 16.12–13). Likewise the church today journeys onward, sustained by the promise of Christ: 'The Paraclete, the Holy Spirit, which the Father will send in my name, will teach you all things and will make you recall all that I have said to you' (John 14.26).

1. *Formation of the canon*

Guided by the Holy Spirit and in the light of the living tradition which it has received, the church has discerned the writings which should be regarded as sacred scripture in the sense that, 'having been written under the inspiration of the Holy Spirit, they have God for author and have been handed on as such to the church' (*Dei Verbum*, 11) and contain 'that truth which God wanted put into the sacred writings for the sake of our salvation' (ibid.).

The discernment of a 'canon' of sacred scripture was the result of a long process. The communities of the old covenant (ranging from particular groups, such as those connected with prophetic circles or the priesthood to the people as a whole) recognized in a certain number of texts the word of God capable of arousing their faith and providing guidance for daily life; they received these texts as a patrimony to be preserved and handed on. In this way these texts ceased to be merely the expression of a particular author's inspiration; they became the common property of the whole people of God. The New Testament attests its own reverence for these sacred texts, received as a precious heritage passed on by the Jewish people. It regards these texts as 'sacred scripture' (Romans 1.2), 'inspired' by the Spirit of God (II Timothy 3.16; cf. II Peter 1.20–21), which 'can never be annulled' (John 10.35).

To these texts, which form 'the Old Testament' (cf. II Corinthians 3.14), the church has closely associated other writings; first, those in which it recognized the authentic witness, coming from the apostles (cf. Luke 1.2; I John 1.1–3) and guaranteed by the Holy Spirit (cf. I Peter 1.12), concerning 'all that Jesus began to do and teach' (Acts 1.1) and, second, the instructions given by the apostles themselves and other disciples for the building up of the community of believers. This double series of writings subsequently came to be known as 'the New Testament'.

Many factors played a part in this process: the conviction that Jesus – and the apostles along with him – had recognized the Old Testament as inspired scripture and that the paschal mystery is its true fulfilment; the conviction that the writings of the New Testament were a genuine reflection of the apostolic preaching (which does not imply that they were all composed by the apostles themselves); the recognition of their conformity with the rule of faith and of their use in the Christian liturgy; finally, the experience of their affinity with the ecclesial life of the communities and of their potential for sustaining this life.

In discerning the canon of scripture, the church was also discerning and defining her own identity. Henceforth scripture was to function as a mirror in which the church could continually rediscover her identity and assess, century after century, the way in which she constantly responds to the gospel and equips herself to be an apt vehicle of its transmission (cf. *Dei Verbum*, 7). This confers on the canonical writings a salvific and theological value completely different from that attaching to other ancient texts. The latter may throw much light on the origins of the faith. But they can never substitute for the authority of the writings held to be canonical and thus fundamental for the understanding of the Christian faith.

2. *Patristic exegesis*

From earliest times it has been understood that the same Holy Spirit, who moved the authors of the New Testament to put in writing the message of salvation (*Dei Verbum*, 7; 18), likewise provided the church with continual assistance for the interpretation of its inspired writings (cf. Irenaeus, *Adv. Haer.*, 3.24.1; cf. 3.1.1; 4.33.8; Origen, *De Princ.*, 2.7.2; Tertullian, *De Praescr.*, 22).

The fathers of the church, who had a particular role in the process of the formation of the canon, likewise have a foundational role in relation to the living tradition which unceasingly accompanies and guides the church's reading and interpretation of scripture (cf. *Providentissimus: Ench. Bibl.* 110–111; *Divino Afflante Spiritu*, 28–30; *Ench. Bibl.* 554; *Dei Verbum*, 23; PCB, *Instr. de Evang. Histor.*, 1). Within the broader current of the great tradition, the particular contribution of patristic exegesis consists in this: to have drawn out from the totality of scripture the basic orientations which shaped the doctrinal tradition of the church and to have provided a rich theological teaching for the instruction and spiritual sustenance of the faithful.

The fathers of the church placed a high value upon the reading of scripture and its interpretation. This can be seen, first of all, in works directly linked to the understanding of scripture, such as homilies and commentaries. But it is also evident in works of controversy and theology, where appeal is made to scripture in support of the main argument.

For the fathers the chief occasion for reading the Bible is in church, in the course of the liturgy. This is why the interpretations they provide are always of a theological and pastoral nature, touching upon relationship with God, so as to be helpful both for the community and the individual believer.

The fathers look upon the Bible above all as the Book of God, the single work of a single author. This does not mean, however, that they reduce the human authors to nothing more than passive instruments; they are quite capable, also, of according to a particular book its own specific purpose. But their type of approach pays scant attention to the historical development of revelation. Many fathers of the church present the *Logos*, the Word of God, as author of the Old Testament and in this way insist that all scripture has a christological meaning.

Setting aside certain exegetes of the School of Antioch (Theodore of Mopsuestia, in particular), the fathers felt themselves at liberty to take a sentence out of its context in order to bring out some revealed truth which they found expressed within it. In apologetic directed against Jewish positions or in theological dispute with other theologians, they did not hesitate to rely on this kind of interpretation.

Their chief concern being to live from the Bible in communion with their brothers and sisters, the fathers were usually content to use the text of the Bible current in their own context. What led Origen to take a systematic interest in the Hebrew Bible was a concern to conduct arguments with Jews from texts which the latter found acceptable. Thus, in his praise for the *hebraica veritas*, St Jerome appears, in this respect, a somewhat untypical figure.

As a way of eliminating the scandal which particular passages of the Bible might provide for certain Christians, not to mention pagan adversaries of Christianity, the fathers had recourse fairly frequently to the allegorical method. But they rarely abandoned the literalness and historicity of texts. The fathers' recourse to allegory transcends for the most part a simple adaptation to the allegorical method in use among pagan authors.

Recourse to allegory stems also from the conviction that the Bible, as God's book, was given by God to his people, the church. In principle, there is nothing in it which is to be set aside as out of date or completely lacking meaning. God is constantly speaking to his Christian people a message that is ever relevant for their time. In their explanations of the Bible, the fathers mix and weave together typological and allegorical interpretations in a virtually inextricable way. But they do so always for a pastoral and pedagogical purpose, convinced that everything that has been written has been written for our instruction (cf. I Corinthians 10.11).

Convinced that they are dealing with the Book of God and therefore with something of inexhaustible meaning, the fathers hold that any particular passage is open to any particular interpretation on an allegorical basis. But they also consider that others are free to offer something else, provided only that what is offered respects the analogy of faith.

The allegorical interpretation of scripture so characteristic of patristic exegesis runs the risk of being something of an embarrassment to people today. But the experience of the church expressed in this exegesis makes a contribution that is always useful (cf. *Divino*

Afflante Spiritu, 31–32; *Dei Verbum*, 23). The fathers of the church teach to read the Bible theologically, within the heart of a living tradition, with an authentic Christian spirit.

3. Roles of various members of the church in interpretation

The scriptures, as given to the church, are the communal treasure of the entire body of believers: 'Sacred tradition and sacred scripture form one sacred deposit of the word of God, entrusted to the church. Holding fast to this deposit, the entire holy people, united with its pastors, remains steadfastly faithful to the teaching of the apostles' (*Dei Verbum*, 10; cf. also 21). It is true that the familiarity with the text of scripture has been more notable among the faithful at some periods of the church's history than in others. But scripture has been at the forefront of all the important moments of renewal in the life of the church, from the monastic movement of the early centuries to the recent era of the Second Vatican Council.

This same council teaches that all the baptized, when they bring their faith in Christ to the celebration of the eucharist, recognize the presence of Christ also in his word, 'for it is he himself who speaks when the holy scriptures are read in the church' (*Sacrosanctum Concilium*, 7). To this hearing of the word, they bring that 'sense of the faith' (*sensus fidei*) which characterizes the entire people (of God). '. . . For by this sense of faith aroused and sustained by the Spirit of truth, the people of God, guided by the sacred magisterium which it faithfully follows, accepts not a human word but the very Word of God (cf. I Thessalonians 2.13). It holds fast unerringly to the faith once delivered to the saints (cf. Jude 3), it penetrates it more deeply with accurate insight and applies it more thoroughly to Christian life' (*Lumen Gentium*, 12).

Thus all the members of the church have a role in the interpretation of scripture. In the exercise of their pastoral ministry, *bishops*, as successors of the apostles, are the first witnesses and guarantors of the living tradition within which scripture is interpreted in every age. 'Enlightened by the Spirit of truth, they have the task of guarding faithfully the word of God, of explaining it and through their preaching making it more widely known' (*Dei Verbum*, 9; cf. *Lumen Gentium*, 25). As co-workers with the bishops, *priests* have as their primary duty the proclamation of the word (*Presby-terorum Ordinis*, 4). They are gifted with a particular charism for the interpretation of scripture, when, transmitting not their own ideas but the word of God, they apply the eternal truth of the gospel to the concrete circumstances of daily life (ibid.) It belongs to priests and to *deacons*, especially when they administer the sacraments, to make clear the unity constituted by word and sacrament in the ministry of the church.

As those who preside at the eucharistic community and as educators in the faith, the ministers of the word have as their principal task not simply to impart instruction, but also to assist the faithful to understand and discern what the word of God is saying to them in their hearts when they hear and reflect upon the scriptures. Thus the *local church* as a whole, on the pattern of Israel, the people of God (Exodus 19.5–6), becomes a community which knows that it is addressed by God (cf. John 6.45), a community that listens eagerly to the word with faith, love and docility (Deuteronomy 6.4–6). Granted that they remain ever united in faith and love with the wider body of the church, such truly listening communities become in their own context vigorous sources of evangelization and of dialogue, as well as agents for social change (*Evangelii Nuntiandi* 57–58; CDF, 'Instruction Concerning Christian Freedom and Liberation', 69–70).

The Spirit is, assuredly, also given to *individual Christians*, so that their hearts can 'burn within them' (Luke 24.32) as they pray and prayerfully study the scripture within the context of their own personal lives. This is why the Second Vatican Council insisted that access to scripture be facilitated in every possible way (*Dei Verbum*, 22; 25). This kind of reading, it should be noted, is never completely private, for the believer always reads and interprets scripture within the faith of the church and then brings back to the community the fruit of that reading for the enrichment of the common faith.

The entire biblical tradition and, in a particular way, the teaching of Jesus in the Gospels indicates as privileged hearers of the word of God those whom the world considers people of lowly status. Jesus acknowledged that things hidden from the wise and learned have been revealed to the simple (Matthew 11.25; Luke 10.21) and that the kingdom of God belongs to those who make themselves like little children (Mark 10.14 and parallels).

Likewise, Jesus proclaimed: 'Blessed are you poor, because the kingdom of God is yours' (Luke 6.20; cf. Matthew 5.3). One of the signs of the Messianic era is the proclamation of the good news to the poor (Luke 4.18; 7.22; Matthew 11.5; cf. CDF, 'Instruction Concerning Christian Freedom and Liberation', 47–48). Those who in their powerlessness and lack of human resources find themselves forced to put their trust in God alone and in his justice have a capacity for hearing and interpreting the word of God which should be taken into account by the whole church; it demands a response on the social level as well.

Recognizing the diversity of gifts and functions which the Spirit places at the service of the community, especially the gift of teaching (I Corinthians 12.28–30; Romans 12.6–7; Ephesians 4.11–16), the church expresses its esteem for those who display a particular ability to contribute to the building up of the body of Christ through their expertise in interpreting scripture (*Divino Afflante Spiritu*, 46–48: *Ench. Bibl.* 564–565; *Dei Verbum* 23; PCB, 'Instruction concerning the Historical Truth of the Gospels', Introd.). Although their labours did not always receive in the past the encouragement that is given them today, exegetes who offer their learning as a service to the church find that they are part of a rich tradition which stretches from the first centuries, with Origen and Jerome, up to more recent times, with Père Lagrange and others, and continues right up to our time. In particular, the discovery of the literal sense of scripture, upon which there is now so much insistence, requires the combined efforts of those who have expertise in the fields of ancient languages, of history and culture, of textual criticism and the analysis of literary forms, and who know how to make good use of the methods of scientific criticism.

Beyond this attention to the text in its original historical context, the church depends on exegetes, animated by the same Spirit as inspired scripture, to ensure that 'there be as great a number of servants of the word of God as possible capable of effectively providing the people of God with the nourishment of the scriptures' (*Divino Afflante Spiritu*, 24; 53–55: *Ench. Bibl.*, 551, 567; *Dei Verbum*, 23; Paul VI, *Sedula Cura* [1971]). A particular cause for satisfaction in our times is the growing number of *women exegetes*; they frequently contribute new and penetrating insights to the interpretation of scripture and rediscover features which had been forgotten.

If, as noted above, the scriptures belong to the entire church and are part of 'the heritage of the faith', which all, pastors and faithful, 'preserve, profess and put into practice in a communal effort', it nevertheless remains true that 'responsibility for authentically interpreting the word of God, as transmitted by scripture and tradition, has been entrusted solely to the living magisterium of the church, which exercises its authority in the name of Jesus Christ' (*Dei Verbum*, 10).

Thus, in the last resort it is the magisterium which has the responsibility of guaranteeing the authenticity of interpretation and, should the occasion arise, of pointing out instances where any particular interpretation is incompatible with the authentic gospel. It discharges this function within the *koinonia* of the body, expressing officially the faith of the church, as a service to the church; to this end it consults theologians, exegetes and other experts, whose legitimate liberty it recognizes and with whom it remains united by reciprocal relationship in the common goal of 'preserving the people of God in the truth which sets them free' (CDF, 'Instruction Concerning the Ecclesial Vocation of the Theologian', 21).

C. The task of the exegete

The task of Catholic exegetes embraces many aspects. It is an ecclesial task, for it consists in the study and explanation of holy scripture in a way that makes all its riches available to pastors and the faithful. But it is at the same time a work of scholarship, which places the Catholic exegete in contact with non-Catholic colleagues and with many areas of scholarly research. Moreover, this task includes at the same time both research and teaching. And each of these normally leads to publication.

1. Principal guidelines

In devoting themselves to their task, Catholic exegetes have to pay due account to the historical character of biblical revelation. For the two testaments express in human words bearing the stamp of their time the historical revelation communicated by God in various ways concerning himself and his plan of salvation. Consequently, exegetes have to make use of the historical-critical method. They cannot, however, accord to it a sole validity. All methods pertaining to the interpretation of texts are entitled to make their contribution to the exegesis of the Bible.

In their work of interpretation Catholic exegetes must never forget that what they are interpreting is the word of God. Their common task is not finished when they have simply determined sources, defined forms or explained literary procedures. They arrive at the true goal of their work only when they have explained the meaning of the biblical text as God's word for today. To this end, they must take into consideration the various hermeneutical perspectives which help toward grasping the contemporary meaning of the biblical message and which make it responsive to the needs of those who read scripture today.

Exegetes should also explain the christological, canonical and ecclesial meanings of the biblical texts.

The *christological* significance of biblical texts is not always evident; it must be made clear whenever possible. Although Christ established the New Covenant in his blood, the books of the First Covenant have not lost their value. Assumed into the proclamation of the Gospel, they acquire and display their full meaning in the 'mystery of Christ' (Ephesians 3.4); they shed light upon multiple aspects of this mystery, while in turn being illuminated by it themselves. These writings, in fact, served to prepare the people of God for his coming (cf. *Dei Verbum*, 14–16).

Although each book of the Bible was written with its own particular end in view and has its own specific meaning, it takes on a deeper meaning when it becomes part of the *canon* as a whole. The exegetical task includes therefore bringing out the truth of Augustine's dictum: '*Novum Testamentum in Vetere latet, et in Novo Vetus patet*' ('The New Testament lies hidden in the Old, and the Old becomes clear in the New') (cf. *Quaest. in Hept*, 2, 73: Collected Works of Latin Church Writers, 28, III, 3, p. 141).

Exegetes have also to explain the relationship that exists between the Bible and the *church*. The Bible came into existence within believing communities. In it the faith of Israel found expression, later that of the early Christian communities. United to the living tradition which preceded it, which accompanies it and is nourished by it (cf. *Dei Verbum*, 21), the Bible is the privileged means which God uses yet again in our own day to shape the building up and the growth of the church as the people of God. This ecclesial dimension necessarily involves an openness to ecumenism.

Moreover, since the Bible tells of God's offer of salvation to all people, the exegetical task necessarily includes a universal dimension. This means taking account of other religions and of the hopes and fears of the world of today.

2. *Research*

The exegetical task is far too large to be successfully pursued by individual scholars working alone. It calls for a division of labour, especially in research, which demands specialists in different fields. Interdisciplinary collaboration will help overcome any limitations that specialization may tend to produce.

It is very important for the good of the entire church, as well as for its influence in the modern world, that a sufficient number of well-prepared persons be committed to research in the various fields of exegetical study. In their concern for the more immediate needs of the ministry, bishops and religious superiors are often tempted not to take sufficiently seriously the responsibility incumbent upon them to make provision for this fundamental need. But a lack in this area exposes the church to serious harm, for pastors and the faithful then run the risk of being at the mercy of an exegetical scholarship which is alien to the church and lacks relationship to the life of faith.

In stating that 'the study of sacred scripture' should be 'as it were the soul of theology' (*Dei Verbum*, 24), the Second Vatican Council has indicated the crucial importance of exegetical research. By the same token, the council has also implicitly reminded Catholic exegetes that their research has an essential relationship to theology, their awareness of which must also be evident.

3. *Teaching*

The declaration of the Council made equally clear the fundamental role which belongs to the teaching of exegesis in the faculties of theology, the seminaries and the religious houses of studies. It is obvious that the level of these studies will not be the same in all cases. It is desirable that the teaching of exegesis be carried out by both men and women. More technical in university faculties, this teaching will have a more directly pastoral orientation in seminaries. But it can never be without an intellectual dimension that is truly serious. To proceed otherwise would be to show disrespect toward the word of God.

Professors of exegesis should communicate to their students a profound appreciation of sacred scripture, showing how it deserves the kind of attentive and objective study which will allow a better appreciation of its literary, historical, social and theological value. They cannot rest content simply with the conveying of a series of facts to be passively absorbed, but should give a genuine introduction to exegetical method, explaining the principal steps, so that students will be in a position to exercise their own personal judgment.

Given the limited time at a teacher's disposal, it is appropriate to make use of two alternative modes of teaching: on the one hand, a synthetic exposition to introduce the student to the study of whole books of the Bible, omitting no important area of the Old or New Testament; on the other hand, in-depth analyses of certain well-chosen texts, which will provide at the same time an introduction to the practice of exegesis. In either case, care must be taken to avoid a onesided approach that would restrict itself, on the one hand, to a spiritual commentary empty of historical-critical grounding or, on the other, to a historical-critical commentary lacking doctrinal or spiritual content (cf. *Divino Afflante Spiritu: Ench. Bibl.* 551–552; PCB, *De Sacra Scriptura Recte Docenda: Ench. Bibl.* 598). Teaching should at one and the same time show forth the historical roots of the biblical writings, the way in which they constitute the personal word of the heavenly Father addressing his children with love (cf. *Dei Verbum*,, 21) and their indispensable role in the pastoral ministry (cf. II Timothy 3.16).

4. Publications

As the fruit of research and a complement to teaching, publications play a highly important role in the advancement and spread of exegetical work. Beyond printed texts, publication today embraces other more powerful and more rapid means of communication (radio, television, other electronic media); it is very advantageous to know how to make use of these things.

For those engaged in research, publication at a high academic level is the principal means of dialogue, discussion and co-operation. Through it, Catholic exegesis can interact with other centres of exegetical research as well as with the scholarly world in general.

There is another form of publication, more short-term in nature, which renders a very great service by its ability to adapt itself to a variety of readers, from the well-educated to children of catechism age, reaching biblical groups, apostolic movements and religious congregations. Exegetes who have a gift for popularization provide an extremely useful and fruitful work, one that is indispensable if the fruit of exegetical studies is to be dispersed as widely as need demands. In this area, the need to make the biblical message something real for today is ever more obvious. This requires that exegetes take into consideration the reasonable demands of educated and cultured persons of our time, clearly distinguishing for their benefit what in the Bible is to be regarded as secondary detail conditioned by a particular age, what must be interpreted as the language of myth and what is to be regarded as the true historical and inspired meaning. The biblical writings were not composed in modern language nor in the style of the twentieth century. The forms of expression and literary genres employed in the Hebrew, Aramaic or Greek text must be made meaningful to men and women of today, who otherwise would be tempted to lose all interest in the Bible or else to interpret it in a simplistic way that is literalist or simply fanciful.

In all this variety of tasks, the Catholic exegete has no other purpose than the service of the word of God. The aim of the exegete is not to substitute for the biblical texts the results of his or her work, whether that involves the reconstruction of ancient sources used by the inspired authors or up-to-date presentation of the latest conclusions of exegetical science. On the contrary, the aim of the exegete is to shed more and more light on the biblical texts themselves, helping them to be better appreciated for what they are in themselves and understood with ever more historical accuracy and spiritual depth.

D. Relationship with other theological disciplines

Being itself a theological discipline, '*fides quaerens intellectum*', exegesis has close and complex relationships with other fields of theological learning. On the one hand, systematic theology has an influence upon the presuppositions with which exegetes approach biblical texts. On the other hand, exegesis provides the other theological disciplines with data fundamental for their operation. There is, accordingly, a relationship of dialogue between exegesis and the other branches of theology, granted always a mutual respect for that which is specific to each.

1. Theology and presuppositions regarding biblical texts

Exegetes necessarily bring certain presuppositions (Fr., *précompre-hension*) to biblical writings. In the case of the Catholic exegete, it is a question of presuppositions based on the certainties of faith: the Bible is a text inspired by God, entrusted to the church for the nurturing of faith and guidance of the Christian life. These certainties of faith do not come to an exegete in an unrefined, raw state, but only as developed in the ecclesial community through the process of theological reflection. The reflection undertaken by systematic theologians upon the inspiration of scripture and the function it serves in the life of the church provides in this way direction for exegetical research.

But correspondingly, the work of exegetes on the inspired texts provides them with an experience which systematic theologians should take into account as they seek to explain more clearly the theology of scriptural inspiration and the interpretation of the Bible within the church. Exegesis creates, in particular, a more lively and precise awareness of the historical character of biblical inspiration. It shows that the process of inspiration is historical, not only because it took place over the course of the history of Israel and of the early church, but also because it came about through the agency of human beings, all of them conditioned by their time and all, under the guidance of the Spirit, playing an active role in the life of the people of God.

Moreover, theology's affirmation of the strict relationship between inspired scripture and tradition has been both confirmed and made more precise through the advance of exegetical study, which has led exegetes to pay increasing attention to the influence upon texts of the life-setting (*Sitz im Leben*) out of which they were formed.

2. *Exegesis and systematic theology*

Without being the sole *locus theologicus*, sacred scripture provides the privileged foundation of theological studies. In order to interpret scripture with scholarly accuracy and precision, theologians need the work of exegetes. From their side, exegetes must orientate their research in such fashion that 'the study of sacred scripture' can be in reality 'as it were the soul of theology' (*Dei Verbum*, 24). To achieve this, they ought to pay particular attention to the religious content of the biblical writings.

Exegetes can help systematic theologians avoid two extremes: on the one hand, a dualism, which would completely separate a doctrinal truth from its linguistic expression, as though the latter were of no importance; on the other hand, a fundamentalism, which, confusing the human and the divine, would consider even the contingent features of human discourse to be revealed truth.

To avoid these two extremes, it is necessary to make distinctions without at the same time making separations – thus to accept a continuing tension. The word of God finds expression in the work of human authors. The thought and the words belong at one and the same time both to God and to human beings, in such a way that the whole Bible comes at once from God and from the inspired human author. This does not mean, however, that God has given the historical conditioning of the message a value which is absolute. It is open both to interpretation and to being brought up to date – which means being detached, to some extent, from its historical conditioning in the past and being transplanted into the historical conditioning of the present. The exegete performs the groundwork for this operation, which the systematic theologians continues by taking into account the other *loci theologici* which contribute to the development of dogma.

3. Exegesis and moral theology

Similar observations can be made regarding the relationship between exegesis and moral theology. The Bible closely links many instructions about proper conduct – commandments, prohibitions, legal prescriptions, prophetic exhortations and accusations, counsels of wisdom, and so forth – to the stories concerning the history of salvation. One of the tasks of exegesis consists in preparing the way for the work of moralists by assessing the significance of this wealth of material.

This task is not simple, for often the biblical texts are not concerned to distinguish universal moral principles from particular prescriptions of ritual purity and legal ordinances. All is mixed together. On the other hand, the Bible reflects a considerable moral development, which finds its completion in the New Testament. It is not sufficient therefore that the Old Testament should indicate a certain moral position (e.g. the practice of slavery or of divorce, or that of extermination in the case of war) for this position to continue to have validity. One has to undertake a process of discernment. This will review the issue in the light of the progress in moral understanding and sensitivity that has occurred over the years.

The writings of the Old Testament contain certain 'imperfect and provisional' elements (*Dei Verbum*, 15), which the divine pedagogy could not eliminate right away. The New Testament itself is not easy to interpret in the area of morality, for it often makes use of imagery, frequently in a way that is paradoxical or even provocative; moreover, in the New Testament area the relationship between Christians and the Jewish Law is the subject of sharp controversy.

Moral theologians therefore have a right to put to exegetes many questions which will stimulate exegetical research. In many cases the response may be that no biblical text explicitly addresses the problem proposed. But even when such is the case, the witness of the Bible, taken within the framework of the forceful dynamic that governs it as a whole, will certainly indicate a fruitful direction to follow. On the most important points the moral principles of the Decalogue remain basic. The Old Testament already contains the principles and the values which require conduct in full conformity with the dignity of the human person, created 'in the image of God' (Genesis 1.27). Through the revelation of God's love that comes in Christ, the New Testament sheds the fullest light upon these principles and values.

4. *Differing points of view and necessary interaction*

In its 1988 document on the interpretation of theological truths, the International Theological Commission recalled that a conflict has broken out in recent times between exegesis and dogmatic theology; it then notes the positive contribution modern exegesis has made to systematic theology ('The Interpretation of Theological Truths', 1988, C.I, 2). To be more precise, it should be said that the conflict was provoked by liberal exegesis. There was no conflict in a generalized sense between Catholic exegesis and dogmatic theology, but only some instances of strong tension. It remains true, however, that tension can degenerate into conflict when, from one side or the other, differing points of view, quite legitimate in themselves, become hardened to such an extent that they become in fact irreconcilable opposites.

The points of view of both disciplines are in fact different and rightly so. The primary task of the exegete is to determine as accurately as possible the meaning of biblical texts in their own proper context, that is, first of all, in their particular literary and historical context and then in the context of the wider canon of scripture. In the course of carrying out this task, the exegete expounds the theological meaning of texts when such a meaning is present. This paves the way for a relationship of continuity between exegesis and further theological reflection. But the point of view is not the same, for the work of the exegete is fundamentally historical and descriptive and restricts itself to the interpretation of the Bible.

Theologians as such have a role that is more speculative and more systematic in nature. For this reason, they are really interested only in certain texts and aspects of the Bible and deal, besides, with much other data which is not biblical – patristic writings, conciliar definitions, other documents of the magisterium, the liturgy – as well as systems of philosophy and the cultural, social and political situation of the contemporary world. Their task is not simply to interpret the Bible; their aim is to present an understanding of the Christian faith that bears the mark of a full reflection upon all its aspects and especially that of its crucial relationship to human existence.

Because of its speculative and systematic orientation, theology has often yielded to the temptation to consider the Bible as a store of *dicta probantia* serving to confirm doctrinal theses. In recent times theologians have become more keenly conscious of the importance of the literary and historical context for the correct interpretation of ancient texts, and they are much more ready to work in collaboration with exegetes.

Inasmuch as it is the word of God set in writing, the Bible has a richness of meaning that no one systematic theology can ever completely capture or confine. One of the principal functions of the Bible is to mount serious challenges to theological systems and to draw attention constantly to the existence of important aspects of divine revelation and human reality which have at times been forgotten or neglected in efforts at systematic reflection. The renewal that has taken place in exegetical methodology can make its own contribution to awareness in these areas.

In a corresponding way, exegesis should allow itself to be informed by theological research. This will prompt it to put important questions to texts and so discover their full meaning and richness. The critical study of the Bible cannot isolate itself from theological research, nor from spiritual experience and the discernment of the church. Exegesis produces its best results when it is carried out in the context of the living faith of the Christian community, which is directed toward the salvation of the entire world.

IV

Interpretation of the Bible in the Life of the Church

Exegetes may have a distinctive role in the interpretation of the Bible but they do not exercise a monopoly. This activity within the church has aspects which go beyond the academic analysis of texts. The church, indeed, does not regard the Bible simply as a collection of historical documents dealing with its own origins – it receives the Bible as word of God, addressed both to itself and to the entire world at the present time. This conviction, stemming from the faith, leads in turn to the work of actualizing and inculturating the biblical message, as well as to various uses of the inspired text in liturgy, in '*lectio divina*', in pastoral ministry and in the ecumenical movement.

A. Actualization

Already within the Bible itself – as we noted in the previous chapter – one can point to instances of actualization: very early texts have been reread in the light of new circumstances and applied to the contemporary situation of the people of God. The same basic conviction necessarily stimulates believing communities of today to continue the process of actualization.

1. Principles

Actualization rests on the following basic principles:

Actualization is possible because the richness of meaning contained in the biblical text gives it a value for all time and all cultures (cf. Isaiah 40.8; 66.18–21; Matthew 28.19–20). The biblical message can at the same time both relativize and enrich the value systems and norms of behaviour of each generation.

Actualization is necessary because, although their message is of lasting value, the biblical texts have been composed with respect to circumstances of the past and in language conditioned by a variety of times and seasons. To reveal their significance for men and women of today, it is necessary to apply their message to contemporary circumstances and to express it in language adapted to the present time. This presupposes a hermeneutical endeavour, the aim of which is to go beyond the historical conditioning so as to determine the essential points of the message.

The work of actualization should always be conscious of the complex relationships that exist in the Christian Bible between the two testaments, since the New Testament presents itself, at one and the same time, as both the fulfilment and the surpassing of the Old. Actualization takes place in line with the dynamic unity thus established.

It is the living tradition of the community of faith that stimulates the task of actualization. This community places itself in explicit continuity with the communities which gave rise to scripture and which preserved and handed it on. In the process of actualization, tradition plays a double role: on the one hand, it provides protection against deviant interpretations; on the other hand, it ensures the transmission of the original dynamism.

Actualization, therefore, cannot mean manipulation of the text. It is not a matter of projecting novel opinions or ideologies upon the biblical writings, but of sincerely seeking to discover what the text has to say at the present time. The text of the Bible has authority over the Christian church at all times, and, although centuries have passed since the time of its composition, the text retains its role of privileged guide not open to manipulation. The magisterium of the church 'is not above the word of God, but serves it, teaching only what has been handed on; by divine commission, with the help of the Holy Spirit, the church listens to the text with love, watches over it in holiness and explains it faithfully' (*Dei Verbum*, 10).

2. Methods

Based on these principles, various methods of actualization are available.

Actualization, already practised within the Bible itself, was continued in the Jewish tradition through proccdurcs found in the Targums and Midrashim: searching for parallel passages (*gezerah shawah*), modification in the reading of the text (*'al tiqrey*), appropriation of a second meaning (*tartey mishma'*), etc.

In their turn, the fathers of the church made use of typology and allegory in order to actualize the biblical text in a manner appropriate to the situation of Christians of their time.

Modern attempts at actualization should keep in mind both changes in ways of thinking and the progress made in interpretative method.

Actualization presupposes a correct exegesis of the text, part of which is the determining of its literal sense. Persons engaged in the work of actualization who do not themselves have training in exegetical procedures should have recourse to good introductions to scripture; this will ensure that their interpretation proceeds in the right direction.

The most sure and promising method for arriving at a successful actualization is the interpretation of scripture by scripture, especially in the case of the texts of the Old Testament which have been reread in the Old Testament itself (e.g., the manna of Exodus 16 in Wisdom 16.20–29) and/or in the New Testament (John 6). The actualization of a biblical text in Christian life will proceed correctly only in relation to the mystery of Christ and of the church. It would be inappropriate, for example, to propose to Christians as models of a struggle for liberation episodes drawn solely from the Old Testament (Exodus; I–II Maccabees).

Based upon various forms of the philosophy of hermeneutics, the task of interpretation involves, accordingly, three steps: (1) to hear the word from within one's own concrete situation; (2) to identify the aspects of the present situation highlighted or put in question by the biblical text; (3) to draw from the fullness of meaning contained in the biblical text those elements capable of advancing the present situation in a way that is productive and consonant with the saving will of God in Christ.

By virtue of actualization, the Bible can shed light upon many current issues: for example, the question of various forms of ministry, the sense of the church as communion, the preferential option for the poor, liberation theology, the situation of women. Actualization can also attend to values of which the modern world is more and more conscious, such as the rights of the human person, the protection of human life, the preservation of nature, the longing for world peace.

3. Limits

So as to remain in agreement with the saving truth expressed in the Bible, the process of actualization should keep within certain limits and be careful not to take wrong directions.

While every reading of the Bible is necessarily selective, care should be taken to avoid tendentious interpretations, that is, readings which, instead of being docile to the text make use of it only for their own narrow purposes (as is the case in the actualization practised by certain sects, for example Jehovah's Witnesses).

Actualization loses all validity if it is grounded in theoretical principles which are at variance with the fundamental orientations of the biblical text as, for example, a rationalism which is opposed to faith or an atheistic materialism.

Clearly to be rejected also is every attempt at actualization set in a direction contrary to evangelical justice and charity, such as, for example, the use of the Bible to justify racial segregation, anti-semitism or sexism whether on the part of men or of women. Particular attention is necessary, according to the spirit of the Second Vatican Council (*Nostra Aetate*, 4), to avoid absolutely any actualization of certain texts of the New Testament which could provoke or reinforce unfavourable attitudes to the Jewish people. The tragic events of the past must, on the contrary, impel all to keep unceasingly in mind that, according to the New Testament, the Jews remain 'beloved' of God, 'since the gifts and calling of God are irrevocable' (Romans 11.28–29).

False paths will be avoided if actualization of the biblical message begins with a correct interpretation of the text and continues within the stream of the living tradition, under the guidance of the church's magisterium.

In any case, the risk of error does not constitute a valid objection against performing what is a necessary task: that of bringing the message of the Bible to the ears and hearts of people of our own time.

B. Inculturation

While actualization allows the Bible to remain fruitful at different periods, inculturation in a corresponding way looks to the diversity of place: It ensures that the biblical message takes root in a great variety of terrains. This diversity is, to be sure, never total. Every authentic culture is, in fact, in its own way the bearer of universal values established by God.

The theological foundation of inculturation is the conviction of faith that the word of God transcends the cultures in which it has found expression and has the capability of being spread in other cultures, in such a way as to be able to reach all human beings in the cultural context in which they live. This conviction springs from the Bible itself, which, right from the book of Genesis, adopts a universalist stance (Genesis 1.27–28), maintains it subsequently in the blessing promised to all peoples through Abraham and his offspring (Genesis 12.3; 18.18) and confirms it definitively in extending to 'all nations' the proclamation of the Christian Gospel (Matthew 28.18–20; Romans 4.16–17; Ephesians 3.6).

The first stage of inculturation consists in translating the inspired scripture into another language. This step was taken already in the Old Testament period, when the Hebrew text of the Bible was translated orally into Aramaic (Nehemiah 8.8,12) and later in written form into Greek. A translation, of course, is always more than a simple transcription of the original text. The passage from one language to another necessarily involves a change of cultural context: concepts are not identical and symbols have a different meaning, for they come up against other traditions of thought and other ways of life.

Written in Greek, the New Testament is characterized in its

entirety by a dynamic of inculturation. In its transposition of the Palestinian message of Jesus into Judaeo-Hellenistic culture it displays its intention to transcend the limits of a single cultural world.

While it may constitute the basic step, the translation of biblical texts cannot, however, ensure by itself a thorough inculturation. Translation has to be followed by interpretation, which should set the biblical message in more explicit relationship with the ways of feeling, thinking living and self-expression which are proper to the local culture. From interpretation, one passes then to other stages of inculturation, which lead to the formation of a local Christian culture, extending to all aspects of life (prayer, work, social life, customs, legislation, arts and sciences, philosophical and theological reflection). The word of God is, in effect, a seed, which extracts from the earth in which it is planted the elements which are useful for its growth and fruitfulness (cf. *Ad Gentes*, 22). As a consequence, Christians must try to discern 'what riches God, in his generosity, has bestowed on the nations; at the same time they should try to shed the light of the gospel on these treasures, to set them free and bring them under the dominion of God the Saviour' (*Ad Gentes*, 11).

This is not, as is clear, a one-way process; it involves 'mutual enrichment'. On the one hand, the treasures contained in diverse cultures allow the word of God to produce new fruits and, on the other hand, the light of the word allows for a certain selectivity with respect to what cultures have to offer: Harmful elements can be left aside and the development of valuable ones encouraged. Total fidelity to the person of Christ, to the dynamic of his paschal mystery and to his love for the church make it possible to avoid two false solutions: a superficial 'adaptation' of the message, on the one hand, and a syncretistic confusion, on the other (*Ad Gentes*, 22).

Inculturation of the Bible has been carried out from the first centuries, both in the Christian East and in the Christian West, and it has proved very fruitful. However, one can never consider it a task achieved. It must be taken up again and again, in relationship to the way in which cultures continue to evolve. In countries of more recent evangelization, the problem arises in somewhat different terms. Missionaries, in fact, cannot help bring the word of God in the form in which it has been inculturated in their own country of origin. New local churches have to make every effort to convert this foreign form of biblical inculturation into another form more closely corresponding to the culture of their own land.

C. Use of the Bible

1. In the liturgy

From the earliest days of the church, the reading of scripture has been an integral part of the Christian liturgy, an inheritance to some extent from the liturgy of the synagogue. Today, too, it is above all through the liturgy that Christians come into contact with scripture, particularly during the Sunday celebration of the eucharist.

In principle, the liturgy, and especially the sacramental liturgy, the high point of which is the eucharistic celebration, brings about the most perfect actualization of the biblical texts, for the liturgy places the proclamation in the midst of the community of believers, gathered around Christ so as to draw near to God. Christ is then 'present in his word, because it is he himself who speaks when sacred scripture is read in the church' (*Sacrosanctum Concilium*, 7). Written text thus becomes living word.

The liturgical reform initiated by the Second Vatican Council sought to provide Catholics with rich sustenance from the Bible. The triple cycle of Sunday readings gives a privileged place to the Gospels, in such a way as to shed light on the mystery of Christ as principle of our salvation. By regularly associating a text of the Old Testament with the text of the Gospel, the cycle often suggests a scriptural interpretation moving in the direction of typology. But, of course, such is not the only kind of interpretation possible.

The homily, which seeks to actualize more explicitly the word of God, is an integral part of the liturgy. We will speak of it later when we treat of the pastoral ministry.

The lectionary, issued at the direction of the council (*Sacrosanctum Concilium*, 35) is meant to allow for a reading of sacred scripture that is 'more abundant, more varied and more suitable'. In its present state, it only partially fulfils this goal. Nevertheless even as it stands it has had positive ecumenical results. In certain countries it also has served to indicate the lack of familiarity with scripture on the part of many Catholics.

The Liturgy of the Word is a crucial element in the celebration of each of the sacraments of the church; it does not consist simply in a series of readings one after the other; it ought to involve as well periods of silence and of prayer. This liturgy, in particular the Liturgy of the Hours, makes selections from the book of Psalms to help the Christian community pray. Hymns and prayers are all filled with the language of the Bible and the symbolism it contains. How necessary it is, therefore, that participation in the liturgy be prepared for and accompanied by the practice of reading scripture.

If in the readings 'God addresses the word to his people' (Roman Missal, n. 33), the Liturgy of the Word requires that great care be taken both in the proclamation of the readings and in their interpretation. It is therefore desirable that the formation of those who are to preside at the assembly and of those who serve with them take full account of what is required for a liturgy of the word of God that is fully renewed. Thus, through a combined effort, the church will carry on the mission entrusted to it, 'to take the bread of life from the table both of the word of God and of the body of Christ and offer it to the faithful' (*Dei Verbum*, 21).

2. *Lectio divina*

Lectio divina is a reading, on an individual or communal level, of a more or less lengthy passage of scripture, received as the word of God and leading, at the prompting of the Spirit, to meditation, prayer and contemplation.

Concern for regular, even daily reading of scripture reflects early church custom. As a group practice, it is attested in the third century, at the time of Origen; he used to give homilies based on a text of scripture read continuously throughout a week. At that time there were daily gatherings devoted to the reading and explanation of scripture. But the practice did not always meet with great success among Christians (Origen, *Hom. Gen.*, X.1) and was eventually abandoned.

Lectio divina, especially on the part of the individual, is attested in the monastic life in its golden age. In modern times, an instruction of the biblical commission, approved by Pope Pius XII, recommended this *lectio* to all clerics, secular and religious (*De Scriptura Sacra*, 1950: *Ench. Bibl.*, 592). Insistence on *lectio divina* in both its forms, individual and communal, has therefore become a reality once more. The end in view is to create and nourish 'an efficacious and constant love' of sacred scripture, source of the interior life and of apostolic fruitfulness (*Ench. Bibl.*, 591 and 567), also to promote a better understanding of the liturgy and to assure the Bible a more important place in theological studies and in prayer.

The conciliar constitution *Dei Verbum* (No. 25) is equally insistent on an assiduous reading of scripture for priests and religious. Moreover – and this is something new – it also invites 'all the faithful of Christ' to acquire 'through frequent reading of the divine scripture "the surpassing knowledge of Christ Jesus" (Philippians 3.8)'. Different methods are proposed. Alongside private reading, there is the suggestion of reading in a group. The conciliar text stresses that prayer should accompany the reading of scripture, for prayer is the response to the word of God encountered in scripture under the inspiration of the Spirit. Many initiatives for communal reading have been launched among Christians, and one can only encourage this desire to derive from scripture a better knowledge of God and of his plan of salvation in Jesus Christ.

3. In pastoral ministry

The frequent recourse to the Bible in pastoral ministry, as recommended by *Dei Verbum* (No. 24), takes on various forms depending on the kind of interpretation that is useful to pastors and helpful for the understanding of the faithful. Three principal situations can be distinguished: catechesis, preaching and the biblical apostolate. Many factors are involved, relating to the general level of Christian life.

The explanation of the word of God in catechesis (*Sacrosanctum Concilium*, 35; General Catechetical Directory, 1971, 16) has sacred scripture as first source. Explained in the context of the tradition, scripture provides the starting point, foundation and norm of catechetical teaching. One of the goals of catechesis should be to initiate a person in a correct understanding and fruitful reading of the Bible. This will bring about the discovery of the divine truth it contains and evoke as generous a response as is possible to the message God addresses through his word to the whole human race.

Catechesis should proceed from the historical context of divine revelation so as to present persons and events of the Old and New Testaments in the light of God's overall plan.

To move from the biblical text to its salvific meaning for the present time various hermeneutic procedures are employed. These will give rise to different kinds of commentary. The effectiveness of the catechesis depends on the value of the hermeneutic employed. There is the danger of resting content with a superficial commentary, one which remains simply a chronological presentation of the sequence of persons and events in the Bible.

Clearly, catechesis can avail itself of only a small part of the full range of biblical texts. Generally speaking, it will make particular use of stories, both those of the New Testament and those of the Old. It will single out the Decalogue. It should also see that it makes use of the prophetic oracles, the wisdom teaching and the great discourses in the Gospels such as the Sermon on the Mount.

The presentation of the Gospels should be done in such a way as to elicit an encounter with Christ, who provides the key to the whole biblical revelation and communicates the call of God that summons each one to respond. The word of the prophets and that of the 'ministers of the word' (Luke 1.2) ought to appear as something addressed to Christians now.

Analogous remarks apply to the ministry of preaching, which should draw from the ancient texts spiritual sustenance adapted to the present needs of the Christian community.

Today this ministry is exercised especially at the close of the first part of the eucharistic celebration, through the homily which follows the proclamation of the word of God.

The explanation of the biblical texts given in the course of the homily cannot enter into great detail. It is, accordingly, fitting to explain the central contribution of texts, that which is most enlightening for faith and most stimulating for the progress of the Christian life, both on the community and individual level. Presenting this central contribution means striving to achieve its actualization and inculturation, in accordance with what has been said above.

Good hermeneutical principles are necessary to attain this end. Want of preparation in this area leads to the temptation to avoid plumbing the depths of the biblical readings and to being content simply to moralize or to speak of contemporary issues in a way that fails to shed upon the light of God's word.

In some countries exegetes have helped produce publication designed to assist pastors in their responsibility to interpret correctly the biblical texts of the liturgy and make them properly meaningful for today. It is desirable that such efforts be repeated on a wider scale.

Preachers should certainly avoid insisting in a onesided way on the obligations incumbent upon believers. The biblical message must preserve its principal characteristic of being the good news of salvation freely offered by God. Preaching will perform a task more useful and more conformed to the Bible if it helps the faithful above all to 'know the gift of God' (John 4.10) as it has been revealed in scripture; they will then undersand in a positive light the obligations that flow from it.

The biblical apostolate has as its objective to make known the Bible as the word of God and source of life. First of all, it promotes the translation of the Bible into every kind of language and seeks to spread these translations as widely as possible. It creates and supports numerous initiatives: the formation of groups devoted to the study of the Bible, conferences on the Bible, biblical weeks, the publication of journals and books, etc.

An important contribution is made by church associations and movements which place a high premium upon the reading of the Bible within the perspective of faith and Christian action. Many 'basic Christian communities' focus their gatherings upon the Bible and set themselves a threefold objective: to know the Bible, to create community and to serve the people. Here also exegetes can render useful assistance in avoiding actualizations of the biblical message that are not well grounded in the text. But there is reason to rejoice in seeing the Bible in the hands of people of lowly condition and of the poor; they can bring to its interpretation and to its actualization a light more penetrating, from the spiritual and existential point of view, than that which comes from a learning which relies upon its own resources alone (cf. Matthew 11.25).

The ever increasing importance of the instruments of mass communication ('mass media') – the press, radio, television – requires that proclamation of the word of God and knowledge of the Bible be propagated by these means. Their very distinctive features and, on the other hand, their capacity to influence a vast public require a particular training in their use. This will help to avoid paltry improvisations, along with striking effects that are actually in poor taste.

Whatever be the context – catechetics preaching or the biblical apostolate – the text of the Bible should always be presented with the respect it deserves.

4. In ecumenism

If the ecumenical movement as a distinct and organized phenomenon is relatively recent, the idea of the unity of God's people, which this movement seeks to restore, is profoundly based in scripture. Such an objective was the constant concern of the Lord (John 10.16; 17.11, 20–23). It looks to the union of Christians in faith, hope and love (Ephesians 4.2–5), in mutual respect (Philippians 2.1–5) and solidarity (I Corinthians 12.14–27; Romans 12.4–5), but also and above all an organic union in Christ, after the manner of vine and branches (John 15.4–5), head and members (Ephesians 1.2–23; 4.12–16). This union should be perfect, in the likeness of the union of the Father and the Son (John 17.11, 22). Scripture provides its theological foundation (Ephesians 4.4–6; Galatians 3.27–28), the first apostolic community its concrete, living model (Acts 2.44; 4.32).

Most of the issues which ecumenical dialogue has to confront are related in some way to the interpretation of biblical texts. Some of the issues are theological: eschatology, the structure of the church, primacy and collegiality, marriage and divorce, the admission of women to the ministerial priesthood and so forth. Others are of a canonical and juridical nature: they concern the administration of the universal church and of local churches. There are others, finally, that are strictly biblical: the list of the canonical books, certain hermeneutical questions, etc.

Although it cannot claim to resolve all these issues by itself, biblical exegesis is called upon to make an important contribution to the ecumenical area. A remarkable degree of progress has already been achieved. Through the adoption of that same methods and analogous hermeneutical points of view, exegetes of various Christian confessions have arrived at a remarkable level of agreement in the interpretation of scripture, as is shown by the text and notes of a number of ecumenical translations of the Bible, as well as by other publications.

Indeed it is clear that on some points differences in the interpretation of scripture are often stimulating and can be shown to be complementary and enriching. Such is the case when these differences express values belonging to the particular tradition of various Christian communities and so convey a sense of the manifold aspects of the mystery of Christ.

Since the Bible is the common basis of the rule of faith, the ecumenical imperative urgently summons all Christians to a rereading of the inspired text, in docility of the Holy Spirit, in charity, sincerity and humility; it calls upon all to meditate on these texts and to live them in such a way as to achieve the conversion of heart and sanctity of life. These two qualities, when united with prayer for the unity of Christians, constitute the soul of the entire ecumenical movement (cf. *Unitatis Redintegratio*, no. 8). To achieve this goal, it is necessary to make the acquiring of a Bible something within the reach of as many Christians as possible, to encourage ecumenical translations – since having a common text greatly assists reading and understanding together – and also ecumenical prayer groups, in order to contribute, by an authentic and living witness, to the achievement of unity within the diversity (cf. Romans 12.4–5).

Conclusion

From what has been said in the course of this long account –
admittedly far too brief on a number of points – the first conclusion
that emerges is that biblical exegesis fulfils, in the church and in the
world, an indispensable task. To attempt to bypass it when seeking to
understand the Bible would be to create an illusion and display lack
of respect for the inspired scripture.

When fundamentalists relegate exegetes to the role of translators
only (failing to grasp that translating the Bible is already a work of
exegesis) and refuse to follow them further in their studies, these
same fundamentalists do not realize that, for all their very laudable
concern for total fidelity to the word of God, they proceed in fact
along ways which will lead them far away from the true meaning of
the biblical texts, as well as from full acceptance of the consequences
of the incarnation. The eternal Word became incarnate at a precise
period of history, within a clearly defined cultural and social
environment. Anyone who desires to understand the word of God
should humbly seek it out there where it has made itself visible and
accept to this end the necessary help of human knowledge.
Addressing men and women, from the beginnings of the Old
Testament onward, God made use of all the possibilities of human
language, while at the same time accepting that his word be subject
to the constraints caused by the limitations of this language. Proper
respect for inspired scripture requires undertaking all the labours
necessary to gain a thorough grasp of its meaning. Certainly, it is not
possible that each Christian personally pursue all the kinds of
research which make for a better understanding of the biblical text.
This task is entrusted to exegetes, who have the responsibility in this
matter to see that all profit from their labour.

A second conclusion is that the very nature of biblical texts means that interpreting them will require continued use of the historical-critical method, at least in its principal procedures. The Bible, in effect, does not present itself as a direct revelation of timeless truths but as the written testimony to a series of interventions in which God reveals himself in human history. In a way that differs from tenets of other religions, the message of the Bible is solidly grounded in history. It follows that the biblical writings cannot be correctly understood without an examination of the historical circumstances that shaped them. 'Diachronic' research will always be indispensable for exegesis. Whatever be their own interest and value, 'synchronic' approaches cannot replace it. To function in a way that will be fruitful, synchronic approaches should accept the conclusions of the diachronic, at least according to their main lines.

But granted this basic principle, the synchronic approaches (the rhetorical, narrative, semiotic and others) are capable, to some extent at least, of bringing about a renewal of exegesis and making a very useful contribution. The historical-critical method, in fact, cannot lay claim to enjoying a monopoly in this area. It must be conscious of *its limits*, as well as of the dangers to which it is exposed. Recent developments in philosophical hermeneutics and, on the other hand, the observations which we have been able to make concerning interpretation within the biblical tradition and the tradition of the church have shed light upon many aspects of the problem of interpretation that the historical-critical method has tended to ignore. Concerned above all to establish the meaning of texts by situating them in their original historical context, this method has at times shown itself insufficiently attentive to the dynamic aspect of meaning and to the possibility that meaning can continue to develop. When historical-critical exegesis does not go as far as to take into account the final result of the editorial process but remains absorbed solely in the issues of sources and stratification of texts, it fails to bring the exegetical task to completion.

Through fidelity to the great tradition, of which the Bible itself is a witness, Catholic exegesis should avoid as much as possible this kind of professional bias and maintain its identity as a *theological discipline*, the principal aim of which is the deepening of faith. This does not mean a lesser involvement in scholarly research of the most rigorous kind, nor should it provide excuse for abuse of methodology out of apologetic concern. Each sector of research (textual criticism, linguistic study, literary analysis, etc.) has its own proper rules, which it ought to follow with full autonomy. But no one of these specializations is an end in itself. In the organization of the exegetical task as a whole, the orientation toward the principal goal should remain paramount and thereby serve to obviate any waste of energy. Catholic exegesis does not have the right to become lost, like a stream of water, in the sands of a hypercritical analysis. Its task is to fulfil, in the church and in the world, a vital function, that of contributing to an ever more authentic transmission of the content of the inspired scriptures.

The work of Catholic exegesis already tends toward this end, hand in hand with the renewal of other theological disciplines and with the pastoral task of the actualizing and inculturating of the word of God. In examining the present state of the question and expressing some reflections on the matter, the present essay hopes to have made some contribution toward the gaining, on the part of all, of a clearer awareness of the role of the Catholic exegete.

Members of the Pontifical Biblical Commission

PART TWO
RESPONSES

The Bible in the Church

Peter Hebblethwaite

The Interpretation of the Bible in the Church, prepared by the Pontifical Biblical Commission, is the most important statement on this topic since Vatican II declared that 'Scripture is the soul of theology'.

It is first of all an extraordinary example of 'thinking in centuries'. The first Pope to set down a marker on scripture was Leo XIII with his encyclical *Providentissimus Deus* of 18 November 1893. He was pretty negative about 'modern' methods of exegesis; but that was understandable at a time when critical liberalism was rampant and was, it seemed, tearing the heart out of the Gospels. Even so, he was much more open than his successor, St Pius X, who set Catholic biblical studies back by at least two generations. On the fiftieth anniversary of Leo's encyclical, 30 September 1943, there appeared Pius XII's *Divino Afflante Spiritu*. Its effect was to liberate Catholic exegetes from the most chafing anti-Modernist shackles. It allowed, indeed encouraged, them to study the 'literary forms' of the Bible. That innocent phrase meant that to understand the Bible you do not have to interpret in the same way a narrative, a canticle, a psalm, a parable, a law-text, a genealogy and so on. You have to respect the *genre* of each.

Then came Vatican II. Augustin Bea, the wily German Jesuit who had worked on Pius's biblical encyclical and had also been his confessor, was made founding president of the Secretariat for Christian Unity by Pope John XXIII. John also revamped the Biblical Commission when he thought that they were behaving like dunces.

Today the Pontifical Biblical Commission (to give it its full title) is, according to Cardinal Joseph Ratzinger, prefect of the Congregation for the Doctrine of the Faith and the Commission's president, 'not an organ of the teaching office, but rather a commission of scholars who, in their scientific and ecclesial responsibility as believing exegetes, take stands on important problems of scriptural interpretation and know . . . they have the confidence of the teaching office'.

The twenty members, marshalled by the secretary, the Belgian Jesuit Albert Vanhoye, are all priests. There are five Jesuits – including the American Fr Joseph Fitzmyer – and three Dominicans and one Oblate of Mary Immaculate. Serious scholars, they are sound, essentially sound, incredibly sound. It is always important for theologians to know how far they can go: in biblical studies, this is how far you can go.

Is there such a thing as *Catholic* exegesis? The document answers firmly 'no' if by that is meant some special method of interpretation not shared by other Christians. Any method will do – provided it throws light on the scripture.

Methods have proliferated in the last thirty years: rhetorical analysis (scripture as persuasive, religious discourse); narrative analysis (stories with a purpose – salvation); structuralism (look at the text 'in itself'); the text-in-its-effect-on-the-community. All are passed in review and judged discriminatingly. Another set of methods uses other disciplines: sociology (for example, Jesus seen as an itinerant charismatic); cultural anthropology (for example, Jesus as a 'Mediterranean person'); psychology and psychoanalysis (for example, the significance of taboo and sacrifice). All these methods can be useful; none is sufficient in itself.

Yet there *is* a characteristically Catholic *approach* to scripture which ties all such methods together. Semantic studies have shown that no one ever approaches a text without some preconceptions. It is as well to be aware of such 'pre-understandings', and dangerous to pretend they do not exist. The Catholic 'pre-understanding' is this: 'What characterizes Catholic exegesis is that it deliberately places itself within the living tradition of the church, whose first concern is fidelity to the revelation attested by the Bible.' In this it is closer to the Jewish tradition than to the individualism of some Protestant exegetes, who feel under no obligation toward a particular community.

A section called 'roles of various members of the church in interpretation' says everyone has something to do – but on different levels. Up there are the bishops who 'have the task of guarding faithfully the Word of God, of explaining and through their preaching making it better known' (*Dei Verbum*, 9). Other conciliar texts add that this is the *first* task of the bishop – well ahead of governing and administering.

Priests come next. Here the document seems to make an unwarranted jump and an exaggerated claim. It says that priests 'are gifted with a particular charism for the interpretation of scripture when, transmitting not their own ideas but the word of God, they apply the eternal truth of the gospel to daily life'. Some priests do indeed possess such a charism. But to say that all do so in virtue of their office is to make nonsense of the notion of charism as special gift. In any case, we all know that not every priest is so gifted. In fairness, one must add that the Commission was merely quoting the conciliar decree *Presbyterorum Ordinis* on this topic.

Finally, individual Christians should read the scriptures so that, like the two disciples on the way to Emmaus, their hearts may 'burn within them' (Luke 24.21). But there is a special category who can respond more readily to the word of God: the poor. One of the first signs of the messianic kingdom is 'the proclamation of the good news to the poor' (Luke 4.18).

Bring on, if not the dancing girls, then the women: 'A particular cause for satisfaction in our times is the growing number of *women exegetes*; they frequently contribute new and penetrating insights and rediscover features which had been forgotten' (emphasis in the text). More on that later.

A crucial question is the relationship of exegesis to other branches of theology. There have been tensions and demarcation disputes. The document stresses both the strengths and limitations of exegesis. For example, moral theology may ask questions of exegetes. 'In many cases', the document confesses, 'the response may be that no biblical text addresses the question posed.' Yet even when the Bible is silent, 'its witness, taken within the forceful dynamic that governs it as a whole, will certainly indicate a fruitful direction to follow'.

The relationship with systematic theology is more complicated. Professional exegetes have to explain the meaning of the scriptural texts. This is an historical and descriptive task. It merely paves the way for the systematic theologian, providing him with building-blocks without doing the architectural job.

The document introduces an exciting new concept: actualization – saying what the Bible means for us today. It is a useful term: the rabbis were engaged on the same task with their Targums and Midrashim (relevant interpretations). This is what all Christian preachers are doing. But it is neither an easy nor a self-evident process. The document points out that the Bible has been exploited to justify racial segregation (as in South Africa), anti-semitism, or 'sexism whether on the part of men or of women'. Evidently there is 'true and false actualization' (echoing Yves Congar's book *True and False Reform*, 1954).

A brisk attack on fundamentalism says that its basic mistake is to forget the historical character of biblical revelation. It 'treats the biblical text as though it had been dictated word for word by the Spirit'. It suppresses the personality of the human authors. Worse, fundamentalism is linked to the 'scripture alone' principle which removed the Bible from the realm of tradition. Superficially attractive, because it offers ready-made instant answers, fundamentalism 'invites people to a kind of intellectual suicide. It injects into life a false certitude.'

Liberation theology offers a kind of answer to fundamentalism, though the document rightly says that there is no one liberation theology and its relations to scripture vary enormously. But its main principle is right: 'If a people live in oppression, they must go to the Bible to find nourishment capable of sustaining them in their struggles and hopes.' Liberation theologians, and more importantly the basic communities whose experience they articulate, far from escaping into another world, read the Bible in the light of their own struggles. 'From this light', the document says, 'will come authentic Christian *praxis*, leading to the transformation of society through works of justice and love.' That is a more positive interpretation of liberation theology than we have so far had from Rome.

Yet the dangers of some forms of liberation theology are recognized. The 'partisan' reading recommended can become one-sided. Direct political action is not the specific task of the exegete. The Marxist principle of class-struggle sometimes rears its

ugly head – though since 1989 it is a somewhat battered head.
Liberation theology lays emphasis on the Kingdon on earth, while
neglecting the transcendent dimension.

There is a similar recommendation for feminist theologians. First,
praise: 'Feminist exegesis has brought many benefits. Women . . .
have succeeded, often better than men, in detecting the significance
and role of women in the Bible, in Christian origins and in the
church . . . Feminine sensitivity helps to unmask and correct certain
commonly accepted interpretations which were tendentious and
sought to justify the male domination of women.'

This sounds too good to be true. It is not just a pat on the head.
But now the shocks. Feminist theology often has recourse to
arguments 'from silence'. Sometimes, therefore, it tends to prefer
'hypothetical reconstructions' to the actual inspired texts.

It raises questions of power and patriarchy. Here, says the
document, 'it can be very useful to the church only to the degree that
it does not fall into the very traps that it denounces, and does not lose
sight of the evangelical teaching concerning power as service, a
teaching addressed by Jesus to all disciples, men and women'. Well
yes, er, um. However, a footnote at this point reminds us that not all
members of the Commission agreed with this statement. Of the
nineteen votes cast, four voted against its conclusion and four
abstained.

Fr Brendan Byrne SJ, an Australian member of the Commission,
explained that 'a solid minority of the Commission felt it inappropri-
atc for its totally male membership to read out lessons in humility to
those who, by reason of gender, do not enjoy similar power within
the church' (Letter to *The Tablet*, 23 April 1994, p. 493).

There could have been more emphasis on Jesus the Jew in the
document. It is a rich vein. Jesus was a pious Jew who came 'not to
destroy the law but to fulfil it'. The gaps in the New Testament – on
ecology, work, marriage, liberation – can be filled in once one
accepts that Jesus' prayer was shot through with Genesis and Exodus
thinking. The document recognizes that 'the church reads the Old
Testament in the light of the paschal mystery'. Yet, at the same time,
'one must respect each stage of salvation history. To empty out the
Old Testament of its proper meaning would be to deprive the New
of its roots in history'.

Finally, a word about that barbarous term 'inculturation'. The New Testament is written in Greek. Consequently 'in its transposition of the Palestinian message of Jesus into Judaeo-Hellenic culture, it displays its intention to transcend the limits of a single cultural world'. And this process is still going on. Inculturation 'leads to the formation of a Christian culture, extending to all aspects of life – prayer, work, social customs, legislation, arts and sciences, philosophical and theological reflection'.

It is still going on. And it never stops. The French Jesuit Paul Valadier points out that Christianity, unlike Islam, has never had a 'sacred language' which you must learn to be saved. It begins life as a translation. So translating and retranslating it again and again, in all cultures, whether in Africa or in the United States, or wherever it may be, with respect for the signs of the times, is the permanent, on-going, never-finished Christian task.

2

An Anglican Reaction

J. L. Houlden

The use of the Bible among Christians these days is bewilderingly diverse. Many ignore it most of the time, hearing it in liturgy and making occasional swoops into it to pick out morsels to nourish the soul or buttress the mind. Others see in it the whole backing of their faith, and are not always aware of the sophistication of the operations they perform as they claim its authority for their beliefs and policies. Meanwhile, in the academic world (which is, be it noted, part of the real world), the study of the Bible goes on unabated, using many different methods and generating substantial light. Its effects in church life remain meagre, and why that should be merits a study to itself. When it does get about, it is usually found both fascinating and edifying, feeding mind and heart: alarm and mystification yield even to delight.

What does the study of the Bible seek to achieve? For many it has long centred on the quest for more accurate and more understandable translations, plus factual information about people and places referred to. It is a quest for 'the meaning' of the text.

In recent years, however, the focus has shifted from the study of the Bible to its interpretation. What is involved here is the recognition that whenever we hear or read the Bible, we are in fact interpreting it: not just uncovering meaning that lies in it but giving it meaning. We usually assume that what (whether after study or not) we take it to mean is what it means. But things are not so simple. Seeing meaning does not depend merely on knowing the sense or reference of words. It depends also on the angle from which you look and what you're ready to see, being the person you are.

All the same, there are common approaches to the Bible, common questions that we want to ask of the text: why and when were you written; by and for what sort of people; intending what effect; using what methods to make your points? In principle, of course, all this is not just to do with reading the Bible: it's true of reading any literature, whether serious or trivial. That's why interpreting the Bible is something that anybody can undertake, and the tools for doing it are available for anybody to acquire. It's also why Christians of all kinds have, in recent times, come to approach the Bible along much the same lines. This used not to be so, because churches were apt to prescribe in advance which interpretations their members could hold and which were forbidden. Where that remains true, whether the authority used is formal or more a matter of group solidarity, then interpretation is limited to certain options. But in the mainstream Western churches, as in Western (and Western-type) universities, it is now accepted in practice that interpretation of the Bible has to be a free-ranging business, if the truth is to emerge. Of course Christians have their own momentum: we are interested in the Bible's meaning 'in which the human word and God's work together in the singularity of historical events and the eternity of the everlasting Word, which is contemporary in every age'. That is to say, Christians must not come to the Bible knowing in advance what it must mean in this passage or that, but bringing a special interest and conviction to their study of the text by all reasonable means and from all helpful angles.

The words quoted above come from Cardinal Joseph Ratzinger's preface to a highly significant document issued recently by the Pontifical Biblical Commission (PBC): *The Interpretation of the Bible in the Church*. The document carries great (though not the greatest possible) official weight in the Roman Catholic scheme of things: the PBC 'is not an organ of the teaching office, but rather a commission of scholars who, in their scientific and ecclesial responsibility as believing exegetes, take positions on important problems of scriptural interpretation and know that for this task they enjoy the confidence of the teaching office'. Not a blank cheque, but the next best thing.

The document is the work of a commission of distinguished Roman Catholic scholars, but a commission nevertheless; so the style tends to be deadpan and judicious. Sometimes one can sense painful creaks where a balancing option has been incorporated and harmony thereby preserved. Only once is disagreement recorded, with voting figures given: a nice sign of life. In fact, beneath the rather compressed language inevitable in documents of this genre, there is here a great deal of vitality. From what was said earlier, it is not surprising that this document, though coming from the heart of the Vatican, could (apart from a certain amount of Roman Catholic tinting) as easily have come from any of the mainstream churches of the liberal West – both in its positive endorsement of all the main types of modern biblical study and interpretation, and in its firm rejection of conservative literalism and fundamentalist ways of using the Bible. People who vaguely suppose that the Roman Catholic Church is wedded to traditional and conservative attitudes to the Bible should ponder the content and even more the implications of this document. It may be that these are more revolutionary than the document itself acknowledges.

Much of the document is descriptive: a succinct but exhaustive and lucid account of the various methods that have developed over the centuries, and notably in the last fifty years, for the analysis and interpretation of scripture. The evaluation of each method is as judicious and broadly based as anyone could ask, as is the assessment of the current need for Christians to use the ancient biblical writings intelligently in making decisions and policies for the present. This is very much a careful statement of how the Bible should now function for Christians who are aware both of their tradition and of the honest demands of the present, given what we now have to recognize and welcome concerning the historical and literary character of the various biblical writings. An Anglican may well feel that in subject matter and in virtually all its content this is a document that Anglicans ought to have produced. It might even have given a broader perspective to our recent debates.

In ecumenical terms, it must be of great interest – and some bafflement – that at a time when the impulse towards better understanding between the churches has suffered from a tendency towards retrenchment and conservatism on many sides, there is patently such wide and unquestioned agreement between scholars of all the great churches (and indeed of none) about how to go about the interpretation of the Bible, with disagreements usually having little to do with denominational allegiance; agreement, that is, on

matters which all recognize as the basic source and subject matter of
faith. Here then is a marvel: it is as if, in this fundamental yet per-
vasive area of Christian construction, there was now a sort of secret
republic which has not yet found a way of being recognized or indeed
much noticed by the great kingdoms from which its citizens come –
lest those kingdoms should turn out to be built on foundations of a
rather different character than was supposed.

There are two critical comments to offer concerning this splendid
Vatican document, both bearing on the marvel just described and
helping to explain it.

In his preface, Cardinal Ratzinger gives a brief history of Rome's
attitude to modern biblical study over the past one hundred years.
He presents it as a process of properly cautious but steady movement
towards enlightenment. Though (it will surprise many) he seems
happy to endorse modern interpretation, where there can only be a
shifting diversity of meanings, he does not mention the fact that in no
single big development, later absorbed, have Roman Catholic
scholars taken the initiative, however distinguished their subsequent
contribution. Nor does he give any sense of the odds against which
Roman Catholic scholarship has often struggled: no mention of the
brutal repression, destructive of scholars' lives, in the early part of
this century. One might have hoped for more candour about what is,
after all, common knowledge. And of course it gives concern about
the system: it authorizes the present document, but who can tell what
it will do next? In this area, the reputation for rocklike stability,
beloved of wistful non-Catholics, is ill-deserved. There is much to
be said for letting truth find its own level rather than subjecting it to
an uncertain magisterium.

Secondly, there is an area of difficulty about which, no doubt out
of an admirable preference for positive thinking, the document is
inclined to be bland and even, unusually, to resort to pious platitude.
But who can blame the commission? It is a difficulty that none of the
great churches has yet summoned the energy to tackle much. And
here, for all its diplomatic language, much of the document could
prove to be a time-bomb. The difficulty goes like this. If you go in for
a historical approach to scripture as a necessary dimension of
modern interpretation, you soon discover that many traditional
formulations of doctrine, and sometimes doctrines themselves, were

grounded on what must now seem erroneous interpretations of scripture. This faces you with a dilemma. You can either adopt a strong view of Providence in the church, producing truths even by what now appear wrong thought-processes; or you can be relaxed about the doctrine in the light of your new understanding of its pedigree. The existence of this nettle is never quite acknowledged in the Vatican document, and it is certainly not grasped; but many readers will see it lurking in the undergrowth.

Finally, we became used, around the time of Vatican II, to seeing the old Reformation divisions somewhat transcended. Here at last the old bogey of 'the private interpretation of scripture' comes close to being welcomed as a guest – so long as he (or she) will dwell within the family. The question is whether the guest will prove to be so importunate that he turns out to be a bogey after all.

3

Three Views from the USA

Paul M. Blowers

The second-century Christian theologian Irenaeus of Lyons once described the interpretation of the Bible as being like placing together a grand mosaic, or like assembling Homeric verses into their correct and coherent plot structure. Gnostic allegorizers, Irenaeus argued, had scattered the gems of the scriptural mosaic and configured them again to form an alien portrait. In rereading the Bible, moreover, they had come up with the wrong story line, one foreign to the church's Rule of Faith, the central dramatic narrative of salvation history that was the very substance of the biblical revelation. What made the Gnostics' exegesis so damaging was not that it was subjective as such, but that its subjectivity was not grounded in the church's perspective. Gnostics were thus fated to telling the world a wholly different story of creation and redemption. For all their hermeneutical sophistication, they had missed the very mystery of divine revelation that permeated the scriptural witness of prophets and apostles, a mystery that could be fathomed only within the context of the church's Christocentric experience and life.

Irenaeus, for all his troubles with the Gnostics, could hardly have imagined the changes in the landscape of biblical interpretation eighteen centuries later. No longer, since the Enlightenment, is it virtually universally presupposed that the church or the synagogue is the primary matrix and context for expounding and appropriating scripture. Today there are many and diverse claimants to the Book of Books, many and diverse interpretative cultures. Historicism may have taken some knocks of late but, as Jon Levenson reminded *First Things* readers in February of last year ('The Bible: Unexamined Commitments of Criticism' (1993)), there are not a few apologists of biblical-critical studies who still, in the name of value-neutral objectivity and good scholarly citizenship, insist that Bible stories are honestly comprehensible only to that academy or guild where they are rendered transparent to the time- and culture-bound ideologies that underlie the texts.

On the other side of the spectrum are literary critics who aspire instead to liberate human subjectivity in reading scriptural texts. Scripture still has a story to tell, but it comes to life, they say, only as individual readers or communities put their own questions to the Bible and, spurning the superficialities of 'authorial' or 'original' meaning as well as 'traditional' interpretations, construct ever new semantic possibilities out of the linguistic stuff of the texts. A good novelist may then be a better judge of biblical truth than a philologist, a historian, or a theologian.

Meanwhile, what words of comfort can be spoken to all those post-modern people (churched and unchurched) who, in the absence of a compelling rendition of the biblical narrative, as Robert Jenson writes, 'simply do not apprehend or inhabit a narratable world'? Who will make sense of their lives and their world in the light of the biblical drama of creation and redemption?

The Pontifical Biblical Commission's (PBC) recently published report on *The Interpretation of the Bible in the Church* could not be more timely. Though it is formulated mainly as a statement on the resources, challenges, and 'mission of exegesis' within the Catholic Church, the report also sends unmistakable signals to the broader cultures of biblical hermeneutics in 'postmodernity'. One signal is thoroughly clear: the church is still the foundational context for expounding scripture and the only promising medium for actualizing the Word of God through new 'retellings' (*relectures*) of the biblical story.

The early sections of the report set out a strategy for accommodating a variety of hermeneutical methodologies without paying exclusive homage to any one. The PBC remains realistically committed to the classic resources of historical-critical interpretation in so far as they can open windows to the ancient communities of faith that both produced scripture and were shaped by scripture. 'Diachronic' interpretation, the treatment of texts from the standpoint of their formation and redaction in changing circumstances over time, continues to provide important insights into the historical constraints on the original intentionality and 'literal' sense of the scriptures.

Yet the Bible is still live communication. The more recent 'synchronic' approaches (literary and rhetorical analysis, narrative criticism, semiotics, etc.), which look at scriptural texts primarily as finished units or structures of discourse, can thus be of great assistance in bringing out the language of persuasion, the storied character, and the symbolic richness of the Bible so as to realize genuine interaction between the ancient text and modern readerships. Narrative analysis, in particular, has not only helped to rescue the Bible from historicism but inhibited the reduction of the Bible to a transparent body of propositional truths (*contra* fundamentalism). It has recovered the imperative, intrinsic to scripture itself, 'both to tell the story of salvation (the informative aspect) and to tell the story in view of salvation (the performative aspect)'.

The PBC report projects a constructive collaboration of 'diachronic' and 'synchronic' interpretation. In the best of all possible exegetical worlds this is the model. Many scholars will nevertheless see this goal as highly optimistic in the 'real world' of biblical interpretation where exegetical battles are waged amid the complex networks of academic guilds, well-defined hermeneutical schools of thought, and other channels of scholarly influence in which loyalties are strong, and in which committed Christian and Jewish exegetes must still practise their craft. A case in point is the interpretation of the Pentateuch according to the Four-Source Theory (Documentary Hypothesis), which was for years largely unchallenged in the academy until more recent literary-critical analysis began to stake its claim. Many interpreters are insisting now that the textual dissonance and tensions within the Pentateuch (the dual creation accounts in Genesis 1–2 are a salient example, but there are many more) need not be explained, diachronically, in terms of multiple editorial sources, but synchronically, by the artistry of authors who, in shaping the narratives, retained the tensions as integral to the discourse. There is no consensus that diachronic and synchronic interpretations can coexist; some biblical critics say they are downright incompatible.

The academy, though, can absorb seemingly countless exegetical differences and the impasses to which they may lead. In the church, where the reading of scripture for the life-giving Word makes the stakes of interpretation prohibitively higher, plurality and diversity of perspectives – among exegetes, between exegetes and theologians, etc. – can bring progress in understanding only because of a shared rule of faith, a common interpretative lens, operative in the ecclesial community. The church, the PBC points out, has the advantage of

> a pre-understanding which holds together modern scientific culture and the religious tradition emanating from ancient Israel and from the early Christian community. [Catholic exegetes'] interpretations stand thereby in continuity with a dynamic pattern of interpretation that is found within the Bible itself and continues in the life of the church. This dynamic pattern corresponds to the requirement that there be a lived affinity between the interpreter and the object, an affinity which constitutes, in fact, one of the conditions that make the entire exegetical enterprise possible.

In its later chapters, the PBC report thus draws upon and further articulates a foundational axiom of Catholic hermeneutics, the presupposed organic interrelation between scripture and the church's interpretative tradition. That relation began within the New Testament itself, as the early Christians 'discerned' their own identity by interpreting the paschal mystery of Jesus Christ in the light of the Hebrew scriptures. It continued in the church's 'discernment' of a full Christian biblical canon. And it continues now in the church's ongoing commitment to 'discerning' the fullness of the biblical revelation in new historical contexts by availing itself of intertextual exegesis, canon criticism, and the history of biblical interpretation (especially the theologically rich patristic exegetical tradition).

The theme of 'discernment' is an important current running through this entire document. Revelation is discerned, not apprehended directly or mechanically. And the authoritative claims of the Bible on the church are not primarily those of law or of dogma. As Sean McEvenue has argued, the Bible's authority is most basically a *spiritual authority*, effective and convertive. Transformation is concomitant with understanding. The PBC report thus recognizes that biblical study and interpretation are completed only in conjunction with 'spiritual experience and the discernment of the church'. 'Exegesis produces its best results when it is carried out in the context of the living faith of the Christian community, which is directed toward the salvation of the entire world.' The closing sections of the report set forth the mission of actualizing, inculturating, and contextualizing the biblical message in the modern world. This missionary focus, however, must be rooted in the continuing consumption of scripture within the church itself – through the reading of the Bible in the liturgy, through the practices of spiritual meditation on scripture, through its use in pastoral ministry, and through the study of the Bible in ecumenical exchanges.

Given the landscape of contemporary biblical studies, Protestants should identify profoundly with the appeal of the PCB boldly to reaffirm the church's hermeneutical prerogatives. H. Richard Niebuhr spoke for many of us when he wrote in his *The Meaning of Revelation* (1941) that

> in Protestantism we have long attempted to say what we mean by revelation by pointing to the Scriptures, but we have found that we cannot do so save as we interpret them in a community in which men listen for the word of God in the reading of the Scriptures, or in which men participate in the same spiritual history out of which the record came.

The PBC report may serve notice across the ecumenical board that the 'discernment' of the mystery of biblical revelation, the unfolding of the full implications of the biblical story of salvation for the church and for the world, will demand hermeneutical courage, theological depth, ecclesial and pastoral commitment, and a spirituality rooted both in the Bible and the Christian tradition.

Jon D. Levenson

Carl E. Braaten has suggested that the foundational assumption of the report of the Pontifical Biblical Commission, *The Interpretation of the Bible in the Church*, is the hermeneutical equivalent of the Definition of Chalcedon (451 CE). Whatever the limitations of the analogy, it is surely the case that just as that ancient conciliar statement affirmed the indivisibility and inseparability of the humanity of Christ from his divinity, so does the Commission's report reaffirm that scripture is the 'word of God in human language', repeatedly insisting that the two natures of the text can never be altogether decoupled.

This, in turn, accounts for a certain two-sidedness in the document itself, which continually embraces modern methods of biblical study but then warns of their limitations. 'Psychology and psychoanalysis,' for example, 'lead to a multidimensional under-standing of scripture and help decode the human language of revelation', but they 'should not serve to eliminate the reality of sin and of salvation.' Modern methods, including even those that originate in secular sciences, can illuminate the sacred text in important, even essential ways, but as the report says of cultural anthropology, they are powerless 'to determine what is specifically the content of revelation'. The resulting report is thus generally one of admirable balance and thoughtfulness. It is also wonderfully comprehensive and concise, a document of great value to both Catholic and non-Catholic interpreters of the Bible.

The divine nature of the text comes from its ultimate author, or, as Joseph Cardinal Ratzinger puts it in his preface, its 'genuine author, God'. It is this dimension that recedes or disappears when the historical-critical method of modern academic biblical scholarship is, in the words of the report, granted 'sole validity'. As Ratzinger correctly and astutely observes, this can result in 'putting the [biblical] word back into the past completely so that it is no longer taken in its actuality' and 'only [its] human dimension appears as real'. This is precisely the effect (and often also the intention) of many programs in biblical studies in universities and even seminar-ies today. How this desacralization can be avoided in academic communities that are not religiously homogeneous is a pressing issue to many of us, but not one addressed in the report, which is, as its title indicates, interested only in *The Interpretation of the Bible in the [Roman Catholic] Church*. Instead, the Commissioin seems to believe that the divine dimension of scripture will be protected if only there is 'full participation on the part of exegetes in the life and faith of the believing community of their own time', if 'church authority [sees] to it that . . . interpretation remains faithful to the great tradition which has produced the texts', and so on.

The fact remains, however, that unless the Catholic Church (re)ghettoizes itself, as I think to be logistically impossible, its exegetes will continue to be integral members of communities of interpretation that are religiously diverse and whose lingua franca has long been historicism and naturalism – that is, philosophical positions averse to the monotheistic traditions and biased toward secularity. If the transcendent dimension of the text is to be upheld without suppressing the human, historical dimension, means will have to be found to prosecute biblical scholarship on genuinely public grounds – that is, on grounds that are pluralistic, and not simply historicistic and naturalistic. How this can be done is an issue as vexing as it is pressing and one on which the Commission offers no help. A schizoid solution – the Catholic exegete as Catholic in church but historicist in the academy – will not effectively redress the recession of the divine dimension of the text that Ratzinger opposes.

It is the frank recognition of the human dimension of the scripture that accounts for the report's stern and repeated denunciations of fundamentalism, which 'fails to recognize that the word of God has been formulated in language and expression conditioned by various periods' and thus 'considers historical everything that is reported or recounted with verbs in the past tense'. As a result '[i]t injects into life a false certitude' and even 'invites people to a kind of intellectual suicide'. Nothing else that this remarkably open and learned report addresses – not even feminist exegesis (which 'has brought many benefits') or Marxist liberationism – comes in for so much censure as fundamentalism. This may partially reflect the gains that various Protestant fundamentalist groups have made in historically Catholic countries in recent years, while Marxism, for example (which has committed literal suicide repeatedly of late, not to mention mass murder earlier), has dramatically lost credibility (except among professors, especially of theology) along with the ability to threaten Rome. But the Commission's eagerness to distance itself from fundamentalism also reflects its conviction that 'the historical-critical method . . . when used in an objective manner, implies of itself no *a priori*' and therefore cannot threaten Catholic doctrine.

The notion of a method without *a priori* suppositions is philosophically naive and easily falsified in the case at hand. One *a priori* of historical critics, for example, is the absence of clairvoyance. Since the Book of Isaiah (who lived in the eighth century BCE) speaks of Cyrus (who lived in the sixth), they therefore must conclude, as did some mediaeval Jewish commentators as well, that the chapters that do so were added late as a *vaticinium ex eventu*. Without the *a priori* naturalism, one could instead argue that Isaiah had a gift of foreknowledge, as befits a prophet (though this would, of course, still not explain the stylistic differences between the various sections of the book that now goes by his name). While I quite agree with the Commission about the historically conditioned character of all texts and the corollary inadequacy of fundamentalism, it seems to me to be evading the tensions (if not outright contradictions) between the divine and the human dimensions that its own *a priori* suppositions ascribe to the Bible.

It also evades the possibility that the 'more precise understanding of the truth of sacred scripture' that the historical-critical method yields can lead to the denial of magisterial teaching. I think, for example, of Father John P. Meier's courageous presidential address at the general meeting of the Catholic Biblical Association in 1991, entitled, 'The Brothers and Sisters of Jesus in Ecumenical Perspective'. The ecumenical issue is simple: whereas the Roman Catholic Church teaches the perpetual virginity of Mary, some communions, following references in the New Testament to Jesus' siblings, do not affirm her virginity to have continued beyond the time of his brith. An extremely learned and meticulous historical-critical analysis compelled Fr Meier to conclude that 'if – prescinding from faith and later church teaching – the historian or exegete is asked to render a judgment on the New Testament and patristic texts we have examined, viewed simply as historical sources, the most probable opinion is that the brothers and sisters of Jesus were true siblings', and not cousins (or half-siblings by some hypothetical previous marriage of Joseph) as some post-canonical traditions came to assert. The question remains, however, whether the 'later church teaching' (from which the responsible historical-critical scholar will necessarily prescind) can be valid when it contradicts the New Testament itself. Could Mary have been a perpetual virgin when the evangelists (not to mention Josephus) not only did not know this but thought otherwise?

The same sort of issue arises not only in regard to divisive ecumenical issues such as the interpretation of Mary or Peter. It also affects basic issues of christology, which the Commission takes as settled. For one of the consequences of historical-critical study is to cast doubt on the assumption that the Bible is, as the report puts it, 'a gathering together of a whole array of witnesses from one great tradition'. On the contrary, this kind of study shows that there never was 'one great tradition' and that the organic unfolding of each stage of tradition from the one that preceded, without jarring disjunctions and flimsy harmonizations, is a chimera. This is a painful thought for any traditionalist (including a traditional Jew like myself), but intellectual honesty requires that it be faced.

Lest the Protestant reader be tempted to feel triumphalistic at this point, it must be noted that those jarring disjunctions occur not only between scripture and tradition but also within each. Indeed, the biblical idea of the Virgin Birth itself, known from Matthew and Luke, is completely unattested in Mark, John, and Paul. The Apostle to the Gentiles, in fact, described Jesus as 'born of a woman' (Galatians 4.4) where an adherent of pious harmonization would surely have expected to read 'born of a virgin'.

When the members of the Commissioin tell us that 'the interpretation of one particular text has to avoid seeking to dominate at the expense of others', they are thus conceding more of their own tradition than they realize. Without such domination, orthodoxy deconstructs. The church can, of course, affirm the fuller traditions of Matthew and Luke to be normative (as it has), but it cannot expect historical criticism to ratify that choice or even to support it. The historical study of the development of texts in the environments that produced the Bible often suggests quite the opposite – that the fuller text has undergone midrashic embellishment and is therefore less reliable *historically* (whatever its *literary* or *theological* value). However deep the personal piety and ecclesial obedience of a historical critic may be, his method compels him to cast doubt on historical claims based on traditions at a significant remove from the events in question. The affirmation of ongoing tradition and the critical study of history are willy-nilly often at cross purposes.

Another difficulty is that the Commission's report handles the Old Testament considerably more critically than the New, on which it tends to fall back into fuzzy mystical language. For example, its affirmation that the 'hyperbole' of 'the royal psalms and messianic prophecies . . . had to be taken literally' after the unexpected death and resurrection of Jesus is more pious than critical. Supposedly, the psalmist's extravagant affirmation that the king's rule will be everlasting (Psalm 45.7) can now be seen to refer to Jesus' endless reign. The problem is this: at the level of *literal* reality, Jesus' kingship, which died aborning, is *more* of a hyperbole than that to which the psalmist referred, not less. A more historically defensible claim is that some early Christians used the mythological language of the old Judahite royal theology to conceptualize their experience of Jesus. The failure of Jesus to return and fulfil the old messianic expectations (despite reports of his resurrection) only heightened the eschatological understanding of the royal theology, already attested in Judaism. The extravagant promises would become reality at the end of time, but not before. On this reading, Judaism and Christianity, despite their irreconcilable difference on the identity of the messianic king, agree on a point that the Commission seems to have missed: the hyperbole of the royal psalms and the messianic prophecies will remain just that until kingdom come.

The treatment of Jesus himself in the report of the Commission exhibits scant influence from the historical-critical method, though the report elsewhere (and, in my judgment, correctly) pronounces it to be 'indispensable'. 'Right from the start of his public ministry', we are told, 'Jesus adopted a personal and original stance different from the accepted interpretation of his age, that "of the scribes and Pharisees"', citing 'his sovereign freedom with respect to Sabbath observance' and 'his way of relativizing the precepts of ritual purity', among other instances. Those intellectually suicidal fundamentalists would have no objection to this formulation, but some historical critics, Christian as well as Jewish, would suggest that since the observance of Jewish law was a hotly disputed issue among Jesus' disciples after his death, it is unlikely that he pronounced definitively against it during his lifetime, and that the passages in which he does so have been put into his mouth by later Christians for polemical purposes. A prime target of the polemic was Judaism. The problem with the report's brief formulation of these issues is thus not only the fundamentalistic assumption that Jesus said what the Gospels attribute to him; it is also that Jesus' continuity with the Judaism of his time (including the Judaism of those patently ridiculous New Testament Pharisees) has been grossly minimized. You would almost think he was Catholic.

Thus, though the report condemns anti-semitic interpretations of the Christian Bible, it seems unaware of the extent to which such interpretations continue certain polemical tendencies within the scripture itself, tendencies that have influenced the portrayal of Jesus. So long as the figure of Jesus is protected from rigorous historical-critical analysis, the danger of anti-semitic interpretation will survive, and precious opportunities for deepening the church's understanding of its scripture will be lost. There is no substitute for the cauterization through historical criticism of the virulent anti-semitic statements that have been put in the mouth of Jesus. Without this, the church's denunciations of anti-semitism ring hollow.

When the historical-critical method *has* been applied to the figure of Jesus, however, it has historically, to one degree or another, driven a wedge between the historical person and the composite literary figure of the New Testament text – that is, between two venerable items in Christian theology, the word of God in human incarnation and the word of God in human language. Perhaps the Chalcedonian hermeneutic is less durable than first seems the case.

Robert L. Wilken

When Origen of Alexandria was preaching on Joshua 7, the account of the capture of the Canaanite city of Ai by the Israelites, his hearers asked him: What does this have to do with us? What value is it to know that the inhabitants of Ai were vanquished, as though this battle was more significant than others? Why does the Holy Spirit include this event and ignore the fall of other, more famous cities? It is a question that is inevitable in a sermon. When the Bible is read by the faithful, especially in Christian worship, the preacher must ask of the text not simply, 'What does the text mean?' but 'What does the text mean for us?'

The new document issued by the Pontifical Biblical Commission entitled *The Interpretation of the Bible in the Church* addresses this problem. Within the last several decades the historical study of the Bible (in its many contemporary forms) has gained widespread acceptance in the church. So great is its hold on biblical scholarship today that its methods are widely assumed to be normative for all interpretation of the Bible. Biblical exegesis is conceived of as a historical and scholarly enterprise carried on by specialists in ancient languages and literature and, more recently, by scholars of social and cultural history.

Yet, argues the Commission, the seeming hegemony of historical criticism is deceptive. 'At the very time when the most prevalent scientific method – the "historical-critical method" – is freely practised in exegesis, including Catholic exegesis, it is itself brought into question.' Even within scholarly circles one can detect mounting criticism of the present direction of biblical studies. But this report is not directed at debates within the guild; it has in mind a deeper and more troubling problem: 'Many of the faithful judge the method deficient from the point of view of faith.' For some, the Commission asserts, biblical criticism has made the Bible a 'closed book', to which the words of the gospel seem applicable: 'You have taken away the key of knowledge; you have not entered in yourselves and you have hindered those who sought to enter' (Luke 11.52).

Strong words these, and they do not come from fundamentalists. These are the judgments of biblical scholars as well as bishops. What is more, the authors of this document are ardent defenders of the legitimacy and necessity of biblical criticism: 'The historical-critical method is the indispensable method for the scientific study of the meaning of ancient texts.' Without the use of historical criticism, argues the Commission, there can be no serious study of the Bible. Its methods have 'made it possible to understand far more accurately the intention of the authors and editors of the Bible as well as the message which they addressed to their first readers. The achievement of these results has lent the historical-critical method an importance of the highest order.'

Fully one-third of the report is devoted to a sympathetic (though not uncritical) presentation of the most widespread 'methods' now in use in the scholarly community: historical criticism; literary analysis (including rhetorical, narrative, semiotic analysis); tradition history; use of human sciences (sociology, anthropology); contextual approaches (liberationist, feminist), et al. The report can and should be read, as Cardinal Ratzinger suggests in his preface, as a confirmation of the 'largely positive' evaluation of historical-critical scholarship found in earlier ecclesiastical documents, e.g., *Divino Afflante Spiritu* of Pius XII (1943), *Sancta Mater Ecclesia* of the Pontifical Biblical Commission (1964), and the dogmatic constitution *Dei Verbum* of the Second Vatican Council (1965).

But the significance of this report is not that it defends the legtimacy of historical criticism. Its timeliness is that it reflects a thoughtful turning away from the easy acceptance of the methods of biblical criticism and offers an argument on behalf of a more theological, spiritual, christological interpretation of the Bible. The report does not claim that historical criticism is illegitimate. It recognizes that the Bible is a book of the past and that it is a fit subject of historical inquiry. What the Commission claims is that a solely historical approach to the Bible has limited usefulness for the church. The Bible speaks not only about the past but also about the present and the future. The question 'What does the text mean for us?' can never be peripheral to the work of biblical interpretation.

Biblical scholarship, however, has largely become a world to itself, divorced from the church's theological and spiritual traditions. For most of the church's history, theology and scriptural interpretation were one. Theology was called *sacra pagina*, and the task of interpreting the Bible was a theological enterprise. The church's faith and life was seen as continuous with the Bible. Even the Reformation appeal to *sola scriptura* assumed that the Bible was the book of the church and its interpretation was to be shaped by the creeds and councils, the liturgy, the theological tradition. For the reformers the christological interpretation of the prophets *was* the literal meaning of the text. In short, the Bible was read within the framework of the church's teaching and practice.

With the emergence of new historical disciplines in the eighteenth century and the application of these disciplines to the scriptures, scholars began, unwittingly at first, to construct a new context to take the place of the church. The aim was to break free of the patterns that had shaped Christian interpretation for centuries. The Bible came to be seen more and more as a book of the ancient world; hence its interpretation was primarily a historical enterprise.

The more the Bible was studied historically and philologically, the more it came to appear foreign to Christian faith and life. It was taken as axiomatic that the scholarly study of the Bible had to exclude references to Christian teaching. The notion that the Nicene Creed might play a role in understanding the biblical conception of God appeared ludicrous. As a consequence biblical scholarship acquired a life of its own as a historical enterprise independent of the church (and of the synagogue). Today its home is the university.

The other Bible, the Bible of the church, however, lives, and, one might add, people live (and die) by it. Scholars will continue to write books about the original setting of Psalm 22 or Isaiah 53, but the Christian interpretation of these texts is fixed in the minds of the faithful and it is not going to go away. The church's interpretation is embedded in the liturgy, in hymns, in the catechetical tradition, and – let us not forget – in the Bible itself. The Christian interpretation of Psalm 22 and Isaiah 53 begins in the New Testament. If one has a quarrel with the church's interpretation of the Bible the debate is not with Origen or St Augustine or St Bernard, it is with St Paul and St Matthew.

It is one thing, however, to recount the limitations of biblical scholarship, quite another to propose a way beyond the present difficulties. The value of the report of the Commission is that it offers a constructive response, one that is firmly rooted in the classical exegetical tradition of the church, yet at the same time attentive to the intellectual developments of the last two centuries. What the Commission offers is a defence of the 'spiritual interpretation' of the Bible. Its arguments are informed, nuanced, and sophisticated, but the very use of the term 'spiritual' will provoke controversy. 'Spiritual interpretation' seems to suggest that the way forward is to go backward, to abandon the accomplishments of the last two hundred years and to return to a precritical reading of the

Bible. From 'spiritual interpretation', some will say, it is only a tiny step to mediaeval allegory and all its evil works.

The Commission is aware of the risks in reintroducing the term 'spiritual'. For this reason it addresses the most obvious criticism of the 'spiritual' sense, namely, that it ignores the historical meaning. Its argument is elegantly simple: spiritual exegesis means interpreting the Bible in light of history, the history of God's revelation in Christ. That is, 'spiritual' means 'historical', reading the scriptures through the prism of Christ's death and resurrection: 'The spiritual sense,' the Commission writes, 'results from setting the text in relation to real *facts* which are not foreign to it; the paschal event [the death and resurrection of Christ], in all its inexhaustible richness, which constitutes the summit of the divine intervention in the history of Israel, to the benefit of all mankind.'

In its zeal to understand the Bible historically, biblical scholarship has ignored the history that is at the centre of the Christian Bible, the incarnation of the divine Logos, the passion and death of Christ, the sending of the Holy Spirit to create the church. Within Christian tradition, historical means christological and ecclesiological. If the Bible is interpreted in this way, it must be read as a book that speaks not only of the past but of life in Christ within the church. The Christian exegetical tradition assumes that what happened historically finds its fulfilment in the present. The writer to Hebrews takes the word 'today' in Psalm 95, '*Today* if you do not harden your hearts', to refer to the present, when '*we* become partners of Christ' (Hebrews 3.7–14). In his great work on the Christian exegetical tradition, *Exégèse Médiévale*, Henri de Lubac, the French Jesuit, entitled one chapter Quotidie, 'today'. According to the spiritual interpretation, that which happened once in the past is made present 'today' in the church's sacramental life and in the lives of the faithful.

At the beginning of his 'literal' commentary on Genesis, St Augustine wrote: 'No Christian will dare say that the [biblical] narrative must not be taken in a spiritual sense.' In support of this he cites the familiar words of Paul in I Corinthians, 'Now all these things that happened to them were symbolic.' But then he gives an example of how St Paul actually interpreted the Bible. In Ephesians 5, for example, Paul quotes the words from Genesis 2: 'For this reason a man will leave his father and mother and be joined to his wife, and the two will become one flesh.' Paul, observes Augustine, gives the text a 'spiritual meaning' by referring it to the church. 'This is a great mystery,' he writes, 'and I am applying it to Christ and the church.'

For Augustine the spiritual interpretation is built on the historical meaning. In the case of I Corinthians, Paul was referring to actual events that had taken place in the desert during the Exodus from Egypt. The 'symbolic' meaning does not displace the reality of the events of which they are a symbol. Likewise, Paul assumes that Genesis 2 is speaking about the physical coming together of a man and a woman in marriage. 'One flesh' refers to a carnal action. Yet St Paul says that this coming together also has a spiritual meaning referring to the mystery of the union between Christ and his church.

Following Paul and Augustine, indeed the church's unanimous tradition, the Commission insists that the spiritual meaning depends on the historical or literal meaning: 'While there is a distinction between the two senses, the spiritual sense can never be stripped of its connection with the literal sense.' Without the prior literal sense the spiritual meaning – or, as some prefer, the mystical meaning – is evanescent. Spiritual interpretation, then, does not mean the imposition of esoteric meanings on the text, but the discernment of the sense that is unveiled by the incarnation of the divine Word and the sending of the Holy Spirit. Three things, according to the Commission, converge in a spiritual interpretation of the Bible: the biblical text, the paschal mystery, and the present circumstances of life in the Spirit.

The mediaeval church expressed its understanding of the spiritual sense in the following distich: *Littera gesta docet: quod credas allegoria; quid agas moralia; quo tendas anagogia.* 'The letter teaches us what happened; what you are to believe is called allegory; what you are to do is called the moral sense; the anagogical sense has to do with the final end of your life.' By dismissing the spiritual sense as a pious fantasy, modern critics have missed the profundity of this verse, and hence of the tradition of spiritual exegesis. For this ancient distich expresses what the church has always believed about the Bible. The Bible records God's action in history (the letter), and it is the task of the interpreter to discern the relation between what is written there and what has come about (and will come about) because of what happened. The three latter senses show how this is best done, by relating the text to what we believe (allegory), to how we are to live (the moral sense), and to what we hope for (the anagogical sense). The God who was is also the God who is and is to come.

The spiritual understanding of the Bible is not a relic from the Middle Ages, a precritical expedient to make do until the advent of historical science. It is the distinctively Christian way of interpreting the Bible. John Henry Newman wrote: 'In all ages of the church, her teachers have shown a disinclination to confine themselves to the mere literal interpretation of scripture . . . It may almost be laid down as an historical fact that the mystical interpretation and orthodoxy will stand or fall together.'

4

A Dutch Catholic Perspective

Jan Holman

No sooner have the clouds of incense around the encyclical *Veritatis Splendor* lifted than the Pope has spoken again, this time through a surprising document on the interpretation of scripture. On 23 April 1993 Pope John Paul II presented this document from the Papal Biblical Commission to the College of Cardinals and the diplomatic corps in Rome. However, it was only released for publication on 18 November 1993.

The occasion for this publication was the centenary of the encyclical *Providentissimus Deus* ('God who foresees all things') of Leo XIII (1893), which opened the door to a scholarly approach to the Bible, and the golden jubilee of Pius XII's encyclical *Divino Afflante Spiritu* ('By the inspiration of the divine Spirit') – the mainstay of modern Catholic exegesis. But the real reason for the recent publication by the Biblical Commission is the increasing tension between the established historical-critical method of exegesis on the one hand and what Cardinal Ratzinger calls the 'panorama of present-day methods' which have attracted attention since Vatican II (1965) on the other.

Origin and status of the document

In his preface Cardinal Ratzinger seems to suggest that the Biblical Commission itself had made the plans for publishing the document. 'The Pontifical Biblical Commission took as its task an attempt to take the bearings of Catholic exegesis in the present situation one hundred years after *Providentissimus Deus* and fifty years after *Divino Afflante Spiritu*. The Pontifical Biblical Commission, in its new form after the Second Vatican Council, is not an organ of the teaching office, but rather a commission of scholars who, in their scientific and ecclesial responsibility as believing exegetes, take positions on important problems of scriptural interpretation and know that for this task they enjoy the confidence of the teaching office.' The Pontifical Biblical Commission itself says that it was '*asked* to make a statement on the interpretation of the Bible'. We are not told by whom. Could it be that here we have a *divine passive*, a grammatical passive form which implies *God himself* as the subject (for example, 'Ask and it will be given to you', Luke 11.9)? Fortunately the Pope clarified the matter in his address of 23 April when he said: 'I accept this document with joy as the fruit of a collegial work which goes back to your initiative, Monsignor Cardinal . . .': Cardinal Ratzinger, President of the Biblical Commission, thus gave himself and his commission the task of producing this document.

According to oral tradition Fr Vanhoye, who was born in 1923, a Parisian with an apparently Dutch name, professor at the Papal Biblical Institute in Rome, a New Testament scholar specializing in the Letter to the Hebrews, wrote the basic text of this document. Of the remaining nineteen members of the Biblical Commission, ten are diocesan priests and nine are priests in religious orders. They are all of sound repute, well skilled in biblical scholarship; there is no doubt about that. But with some exceptions they are not among the best-known figures of Catholic biblical scholarship. However, after about three years of close collaboration the team has produced a document of which the Catholic Church can be proud; we hope that it will serve as a model for the presentation and tone of Vatican documents intended for the world church.

I have gone into the composition of the Biblical Commission in some detail to show that there is still not a single *lay* member of this commission. This is all the more striking since the Catholic Church, above all in the Netherlands, Belgium, Germany and France, is richly blessed with admirable non-clerical experts in biblical exegesis, of both sexes. The document prompts the question why women are absent from the Biblical Commission, which states with papal approval: 'Feminist exegesis has brought many benefits. Women have played a more active part in exegetical research . . . Feminine sensitivity helps to ummask and correct certain commonly accepted interpretations which were tendentious and sought to justify the male domination of women' (above p. 42) and 'It is desirable that the teaching of exegesis be carried out by both men and women' (p. 75). If according to this document women now have so much to offer biblical interpretation, how can the world church allow itself to keep them out of the Biblical Commission without doing itself serious harm?

We have a second unresolved question, namely why this document has not become an encyclical, but only a document from the Papal Biblical Commission, from which moreover Cardinal Ratzinger distances himself a little in his preface ('not an organ of the teaching office, but rather a commission of scholars who . . . enjoy the confidence of the teaching office'). This is despite the fact that both Pope and cardinal emphasize the direct affinity of this document with the encyclicals *Providentissimus Deus* and *Divino Afflante Spiritu*.

Content of the document

A brief introduction sketches out the present state of biblical exegesis. One characteristic feature is the malaise surrounding the most widespread exegetical method, historical criticism. There is a reaction from two sides against this approach which the churches have accepted with much pain and difficulty, and which concentrates on the study of the development of biblical texts over time, a development also denoted by the term 'diachronous' (derived from the Greek *dia*, through, and *chronos*, time). On the one hand, exegetes today are putting question marks against the almost sole domination of the historical-critical method by emphasizing a synchronous (*syn* = 'along with' and *chronos* = 'time') reading of the Bible. This means that they draw attention to the use of language, the structure, the narrative strategies and power of conviction of all kinds of literary features in the biblical texts as we find them here and now (synchronous). On the other hand the community of faithful has clearly indicated that it cannot bake bread to feed its soul from the material which historical criticism offers. Moreover believers who have come of age are asking urgent questions of scripture on the basis of their own experience, as women or as men, in the political,

socio-economic sphere and from the perspectives of disciplines like
sociology and psychology.

The church leaders feel that as a consequence of this twofold
opposition to the historical-critical method there is a risk that the
baby will be thrown out with the bath water. Moreover the result
could be the emergence of a piously intended but theologically fatal
biblical obscurantism. This danger threatens where a so-called
'spiritual' reading of the Bible without any scientific basis enters the
church to satisfy subjective religious needs. To drive out this devil
the new Vatican document surveys the current contemporary
exegetical methods and approaches. As a result it pronounces
positively on them, except in the case of fundamentalism, with here
and there a fatherly admonition about the limitations of particular
approaches. By the term 'method' this document denotes a
collection of academic techniques, and by the term 'approach' it
denotes reading the Bible from a particular (e.g. feminist) perspective. All this can be found in Chapter I, which is very well worth
reading.

Chapter II looks at the sphere of hermeneutics (the *theory* in the
practice of expounding the Bible). Here people like Bultmann,
Gadamer and Ricoeur are mentioned and the relationship between
the literal and spiritual significance of scripture. In Chapter III the
Biblical Commission lists the characteristic aspects of Catholic
biblical exegesis. It is not as though there is a distinctively Catholic
scholarly exegetical method. The issue here is a Catholic preunder-
standing of reading the Bible. This accords tradition inside and
outside the Bible an important place, as of course Judaism has also
done from antiquity. Here we find key words like rereading
(*relecture*), the relationship between Old and New Testaments, the
canon of the biblical books, patristic exegesis, the role of church
government and professional exegesis, and the relationship with
other theological disciplines (dogmatics and moral theology). Finally
Chapter IV investigates the place of the interpretation of the Bible in
the everyday life of the church (liturgy, pastoral work [catechesis,
preaching, Bible study] and private Bible reading).

Critical comments

A careful reading leaves me with a feeling of gratitude for the open and constructive mentality of this thorough document. It tries to talk to the community of faith in a worthwhile way about developments in the interpretation of the Bible since Vatican II (1965). But I would also like to make some critical comments about some things which I feel make less of a contribution to that. The short history of the relationship between church authority and biblical scholars over the past century (above pp. 3f.) could make one think that everything has always gone smoothly. But that is not the case. We need only think of the encyclical *Humani Generis* (1950) and the bitter attacks on the Papal Biblical Institute in Rome at the time of the Second Vatican Council (1963–1964), of which I was an eyewitness as a student.

Secondly, I am struck by the very marked christocentric orientation of this document. 'The church reads the Old Testament in the light of the paschal mystery' (p. 29). There would be nothing against that, were it not that despite all the positive remarks in this document about the Jews, it also inevitably fails to do justice to the intrinsic value of the Old Testament. The striking attention to the mystery of Easter recalls French theology of the 1960s–1970s and some of its German Protestant forerunners.

The redaction of the last chapter (IV) is a bit loose. But any writer facing a deadline can understand this. However, I do find unforgivable the lack of a translation of some Latin texts, and of a glossary with an explanation of technical terms like hermeneutic, allegory, analogy of faith, *hebraica veritas*, *loci theologici*. If the document is addressed to the whole world church, one might expect that the Biblical Commission would also have consulted some experts in communication. A journalist could have helped it to avoid some clerical narrowness.

There are other small blemishes to mention, like the ambiguous expression 'the definition of original sin' (p. 56). The Council of Trent defined *that* original sin exists, but expressly left open to further discussion *in what* it consists. The godfearing Victorian-sounding assertion that 'the Song of Songs was recognized as holy scripture when applied to the relation between God and Israel' (p. 63) seems to me difficult to accept. The remarkable summary of the history of exegesis with the help of the three names Origen (185–255), Jerome (347–419) and Fr Marie-Joseph Lagrange OP (1855–1938) might suggest that French nationalism prevailed over Fr Vanhoye's solidarity with the Society of Jesus. Finally, there is the mysterious and disputed footnote in the last paragraph on feminist exegesis (p. 43), in which the Commission, for all its appreciation, raises a warning finger. The footnote suggests that there was disagreement over this. The four in opposition asked for an explicit mention of their opposition, and got it. According to *Hervormd Nederland* of 9 July 1994 (p. 21), the four thought that 'feminist exegetes do not need a lesson in humility'. But you can also read the passage to mean that these four objected to indicating so openly in the document that there was indeed male misuse of power in the church.

Conclusion

However, I want to end on a positive note by indicating the fact that the heretic Origen (185–255) is the exegete cited most often in this document (seven times). That can give some hope to Dutchmen!

Encouraging and no less hopeful is the fact that this Vatican document uses the term 'dynamic' and derivatives eleven times in contrast to the contemporaneous encyclical *Veritatis Splendor*, which comes over in such a static way.

I hope with all my heart that *The Interpretation of the Bible in the Church* will be used as a guideline for study in many Bible groups, both Protestant and Catholic. And that anyone who takes part in them will say 'Good for the church.'

5

Light on Biblical Authority:
Anglican-Roman Catholic Dialogue

John Muddiman

The Interpretation of the Bible in the Church was published in November 1993, exactly one hundred years after Leo XIII's famous encyclical had suggested that the biblical criticism of the Liberal Protestants might be turned against them, in defence of the church. This was arguably a tactical error, since it sparked off the Modernist crisis and led to half a century of suspicion against even moderate and loyal biblical scholarship. In 1943 Pius XII eased the window open again to see if it might be safe to come out at last. But by 1958, in the twilight of his Pontificate, it was firmly shut but not secured against winds of change unleashed by the Second Vatican Council. These are the landmarks selected for commemoration in the document from the Pontifical Biblical Commission. And they provide a particular reading of the history of twentieth-century Catholicism, its inner dynamic towards a more enlightened view of biblical criticism, which one hopes will turn out to be the correct reading. The content of the document correspondingly seeks to demonstrate the openness and modernity of Catholic exegesis and to celebrate its critical coming of age, by offering a concise and judicious course in biblical hermeneutics.

It starts with a description of the historical-critical method, as 'indispensable', 'actually required' by the nature of scripture, producing results that 'lend it an importance of the highest order'. To be sure it has its limitations: 'It restricts itself to a search for the meaning of the biblical text within the historical circumstances that gave rise to it, and is not concerned with other possibilities of meaning which have been revealed at later stages of the biblical revelation and history of the church.' If this is a criticism, it is exceedingly mild by comparison with the attacks that could and have been aimed at the method by biblical scholars themselves: its massively speculative reconstructions resting on a minimum of evidence; its disintegrating analysis of sources and traditions behind the final form of the text; its Western intellectual presuppositions masquerading as critical neutrality. On balance, the Pontifical Biblical Commission must be reckoned an ally and defender of historical criticism against its varied detractors, using it as a control on the other approaches which it proceeds to outline. This impression is confirmed by the fierce tirade that it reserves for fundamentalism: 'By refusing to take into account the historical character of biblical revelation,' fundamentalist interpretation 'makes itself incapable of accepting the full truth of the incarnation.' It 'naively confuses the final stage of Gospel tradition with the initial' (the historical Jesus), and so fails to appreciate the vital role of the church. 'It actually invites people to a kind of intellectual suicide. It injects into life a false certitude, for it unwittingly confuses the divine substance of the biblical message with what are in fact its human limitations.' (That is, fundamentalism is basically heretical, inherently schismatic and morally perverse.) These quotations clearly reveal the full extent of the Commission's historical-critical sympathies.

Since the Pontifical Biblical Commission now comes under the aegis of the Congregation for the Doctrine of the Faith, the Preface to the document was written by its Prefect, Cardinal Joseph Ratzinger. It gives the text a very different gloss. He draws attention immediately to the 'hidden dangers of historical criticism' as a 'profane' method of interpreting the Bible, and comments that 'the genuine author, God, is removed from reach of a method which was established for understanding human reality'. He explains that 'The biblical word comes . . . not only from the past, but at the same time from the eternity of God, and it leads us back into God's eternity, but again along the way through time to which the past, the present and the future belong.' A different agenda begins to emerge from this carefully wrought sentence. The Bible as word from the past and the development of the church's faith and order through time are here subordinated to the divine decree from all eternity. This is a very different view of the limitations of historical enquiry than those offered in the document.

What lies behind this alternative agenda? It may be illuminating to compare this Preface with the Vatican's 1991 Response to the Final Report of ARCIC I. At several points its criticisms turn on the issue of biblical interpretation, and it develops the point in a concluding paragraph:

> As is well known, the Catholic Doctrine affirms that the historical-critical method is not sufficient for the interpretation of scripture. Such interpretation cannot be separated from the living Tradition of the church which receives the message of scripture. The Final Report seems to ignore this when dealing with the interpretation of the petrine texts of the New Testament, for it states that they 'do not offer sufficient basis' on which to establish the primacy of the Bishop of Rome. In the same way, the Final Report introduces with reference to the infallible judgments of the Bishop of Rome the need for such decisions to be 'manifestly a legitimate interpretation of biblical faith and in line with orthodox tradition'.

It ends by calling for further study concerning scripture, tradition and the magisterium and their interrelationship, on which ARCIC II is currently working.

Although the criticism is phrased in terms of the relation between scripture and tradition, it is the attempt to subordinate in practice both to the magisterium which puts Cardinal Ratzinger at odds not only with ARCIC but also with the Pontifical Biblical Commission. Let us look at the two examples given, Petrine primacy and infallibility, in their original context.

The Final Report (*Authority in the Church* II p. 84), having referred to different interpretations of the Petrine texts in the early church, notes that fathers and doctors gradually came to interpret the data as pointing in the same direction. It continues: 'This interpretation has been questioned, and it has been argued that it arose from an attempt to legitimize a development that had already occurred. Yet it is possible to think that a primacy of the bishop of Rome is not contrary to the New Testament and is part of God's purpose regarding the church's unity and catholicity, while admitting that the New Testament texts offer no sufficient basis for this.' The Final Report, then, rejects the easy sociological explanation, and refers instead to the scriptural norm ('not contrary to the New Testament') and the living tradition ('part of God's purpose') while admitting (to historical criticism) that the New Testament text, in isolation, is not sufficient to establish this view. And the reasons for critical hesitation have been given earlier in the Report: 'The New Testament contains no explicit record of a transmission of Peter's leadership; nor is the transmission of apostolic authority in general very clear' (p. 83). In other words ARCIC accepts the 'well known Catholic doctrine of the insufficiency of the historical critical method'. But the Vatican Response demands more than this, namely acceptance as a historical fact that Jesus himself had the primacy of the Roman See consciously in mind when he appointed Peter as leader of the Twelve, that this belongs to the *ius divinum*, interpreted as meaning 'derivation from the institution of Christ the Lord himself', in the words of Vatican I. Far from respecting the role of living tradition in the interpretation of scripture, the magisterium appeals to the text of scripture alone, as it is privileged to interpret it. Its positivist insistence on derivation from the historical Jesus is quite uncharacteristic of Catholic hermeneutics and is an apologetic over-reaction to those who dispute the Papal claims, similar to the defensiveness of fundamentalism.

The second example on Papal infallibility also needs to be quoted in full. The Final Report (*Authority* II p. 95) reads: 'If the definition proposed for assent (by the Pope speaking *ex cathedra*) were not manifestly a legitimate interpretation of biblical faith and in line with orthodox tradition, Anglicans would think it a duty to reserve reception of the definition for study and discussion.' It becomes clear in context that this is not an agreed statement of ARCIC but a description of an Anglican problem with infallible statements by the Bishop of Rome. When they cohere with scripture and tradition they are afforded assent. But when they do not, as in the case of the immaculate conception of the Blessed Virgin Mary, they are reserved for study and discussion. Now, one could well object to this statement as a piece of ecumenical wishful thinking. Anglicans do not, to be honest, spend a lot of time studying and discussing this topic, even if they understand it. But one cannot fault the logic of the Anglican position. If the magisterium is the servant of scripture and tradition, as it claims, its aim should be precisely to make 'manifest' in its teaching how any infallible statement coheres with scripture and tradition. If, however, infallible statements are to be accepted *per se*, on the authority of the Pope, regardless of their relation to scripture and tradition, then the authority of the latter is fatally undermined. The Final Report refers to 'reception' and speaks later on of the role of reception by the faithful in the process of defining faith and morals. More work certainly needs to be done in clarifying this concept. It is usually on moral questions, rather than doctrinal, such as the prohibition of artificial means of contraception, where reception by the faithful has to be taken seriously. For reception is not, in the end, a matter of intellectual assent but of actual discipleship.

Consideration of two other recent Vatican texts may advance our discussion. In 1992 The Congregation for the Doctrine of the Faith wrote a Letter to the Bishops on aspects of 'the Church as Communion', tacitly alluding to the ARCIC II document of the same title published in the previous year. It discusses the relation of local churches to the church catholic, and warns against current misperceptions. Its central idea is the temporal and ontological priority of the universal church: a mysterious, heavenly reality, which has always retained unimpaired its unity, mediated by communion with the See of Rome as an essential 'internal constituent'. The traditional authorities quoted for this idea are not impressive: II Clement and the Shepherd of Hermas. But there are several echoes of the notion within the New Testament itself. In addition to those cited in the footnotes, Galatians 4.26f. is perhaps the most interesting, where Paul allegorizes Sarah, the wife of Abraham, as 'the Heavenly Jerusalem, mother of us all'. The heavenly church has even more priority it seems than the Letter realizes! Jewish apocalyptic regularly attributed pre-existence to the objects of its eschatological hope; and this is surely the basis of this strange idea. But the Letter consistently removes the future horizontal dimension and is then left with only the vertical and eternal; and it proceeds to apply this to reinforce the conviction of the unchanging perfection of the universal heavenly church, which subsists in the Catholic

Church. We are reminded again of Cardinal Ratzinger's hermeneutical theory: 'The word comes from the eternity of God and
leads us into God's eternity.' An original eschatological idea that was
thoroughly dynamic has been reduced to a static, almost Platonic
timelessness.

Most recently in 1994, the Pope's Apostolic Letter on Ordination
and Women appeals to the unchangeable divine constitution of the
church, in excluding women from the priesthood. 'In calling only
men as his Apostles, Christ acted in a completely free and sovereign
manner', i.e. he was not conditioned by the cultural motives of his
age, so his decision is binding for all time. 'Wherefore, in order that
all doubt may be removed regarding a matter of great importance, a
matter which pertains to the church's divine constitution itself, in
virtue of my ministry of confirming the brethren (cf. Luke 22.32) I
declare that the church has no authority whatsoever to confer
priestly ordination on women and that this judgment is to be
definitively held by all the faithful.' But the problems of biblical
criticism and hermeneutics will not disappear; questions will still be
asked. Are the Twelve simply to be identified as the Apostles, or
were the latter a larger group in the early church, including some
women? Is the choice of twelve men an eschatological symbol for the
imminent restoration of Israel, rather than a blueprint for the
church's ministry? Could Jesus not have reflected the culture of his
time in some respects on any issue, and yet acted with radical
freedom in others? Is the teaching of Christ only authoritative when
it can be shown to transcend its particular Jewish setting? And is
Tradition not a living reality capable of absorbing fresh insights on
how to live the deeper implications of the gospel more consistently?

This paper has tried to point to a serious discrepancy between the
balanced, critical scholarship practised by eminent Catholic scholars
today and commended by the Pontifical Biblical Commission in its,
literally, epoch-making document, and several recent Vatican
statements in reaction to Anglican-Roman Catholic dialogue, which
run the risk of unravelling the ecumenical consensus on biblical
interpretation. To end with a quotation from the document (pp. 93f.):

> Most of the issues which ecumenical dialogue has to confront are
> related in some way to the interpretation of the biblical texts . . .

eschatology, the structure of the church, primacy, the admission of women to the ministerial priesthood . . . the administration of the universal church and of local churches. Although it cannot claim to resolve all these issues by itself, biblical exegesis is called upon to make an important contribution in the ecumenical area. Through the adoption of the same methods and analogous hermeneutical points of view, exegetes of various Christian confessions have arrived at a remarkable level of agreement in the interpretation of scripture.

6

Cracks in the Soul of Theology

Robert P. Carroll

If Jesus Christ is the greatest man, you ought to love him in the greatest degree, now hear how he has given his sanction to the law of ten comandments: did he not mock at the sabbath, and so mock the sabbath's God? murder those who were murder'd because of him? turn away the law from the woman taken in adultery? steal the labor of others to support him? bear false witness when he omitted making a defence before Pilate? covet when he pray'd for his disciples, and when he bid them shake off the dust of their feet against such as refused to lodge them? I tell you, no virtue can exist without breaking these ten commandments. Jesus was all virtue, and acted from impulse, not from rules – William Blake[1]

It is deeply encouraging, on the one hand, to encounter an intelligent document emanating from the Vatican on the subject of the Bible which recognizes the integrity of the historical-critical approach to the Bible and which gives permission for the pious to use such methods by recommending many of the most contemporary approaches to reading the Bible. On the other hand, it is somewhat discouraging to discover that these encouraging features are only surface deep. This is not a critical document which embraces a fully

---

[1] The Devil in 'A Memorable Fancy', Plates 22–24 of 'The Marriage of Heaven and Hell' in *Blake: Complete Writings*, ed. G. Keynes (Oxford: OUP 1969), p. 158. The rest of Blake's statement about the Bible 'in its infernal or diabolical sense' and 'The Bible of Hell' is also important. The complexity of Blake on the Bible is a nice analogue of the complexity of the Bible itself. This Vatican document is too brief to capture much of the Bible's complexity, so to my reading of it I have added Blake on the decalogue by way of introducing some dialectical tension into the discussion.

developed critique of the Bible, incorporating the lessons of the Enlightenment into a mature and reflective reading of the Bible. It is, in fact, an attempt to come to terms with contemporary reading methods in biblical studies while maintaining the integrity of the magisterium in support of a rather traditionalistic interpretation of the Bible in accordance with the dictates of Christian dogmatics. I detect here that ancient game of Jacob dressing up in the clothes of Esau in order to put one over on the blind and unsuspecting Isaac (Genesis 27). The clothes may be the clothes of historical-critical methodology, but the voice is still that of the crafty, scheming Jacob seeking to acquire all the power for himself. The magisterium may dress up in modernist clothes, the old authoritarian voice remains its own. It is still pronouncing on which new methods are acceptable and which are not because they do not agree with the old conciliar dogmatic belief system. So what are we to make of this strange but welcome document?

The new document from the Vatican is only the latest in a long line of utterances about the Bible, starting with Pope Leo XIII's encyclical *Providentissimus Deus* of 1893 and including Pope Pius XII's *Divino Afflante Spiritu* of 1943 and Vatican II's *Dei Verbum* of 1965, but where this new document differs is in its apparent reconciliation of the Vatican with many of the modern methods of biblical scholarship. Throughout the document there is a strong sense of the study of the Bible being 'as it were, the soul of theology' (a phrase borrowed from Pope Leo XIII via *Dei Verbum*, 24). Since Vatican II Catholic biblical scholarship has flourished as never before and Catholic interest in the Bible has become widespread throughout the Catholic Church, especially in its liberationist modes (in Central and South America), even to the point where there are times when the average parish priest begins to sound like a 'bad Protestant' when talking about the Bible. From the point of view of general piety such developments may be a 'good thing', but I would like to offer some critical reflections on this Vatican document as a way of responding to the phenomenon of deep Catholic interest in the Bible and also as a focus on some problems with the interpretation of the Bible in the modern world. Hence my title 'cracks in the soul of theology'.

The claim that 'The biblical word comes from a real past'

(Cardinal Joseph Ratzinger's preface) is the most important lesson to be learned from the modern historical-critical study of the Bible. The biblical documents are historical in the sense that they are the time-conditioned cultural productions of the past. While I happen to think that this fundamental truth of post-Enlightenment thought (another time-conditioned cultural production) is among the most important constructions of Western biblical scholarship, it is *also*, I believe, rather destructive of all totalizing claims for the Bible as being 'the word of God' in some absolute or dogmatics sense. Always the words of the Bible are the words of men and women, whatever later dogmatic systems may have asserted about them being also *the words of God*. While the notion of *some* of the words being 'words from the God' is inscribed in parts of the Bible (e.g., priestly torah and prophetic oracle) most of the Bible is not made up of such notions, so the extension of that notion by later generations to cover all of the words of the Bible seems to me to be an illegitimate totalizing transfer and a fundamental misunderstanding of biblical metaphor and trope. In these matters I am a child of the Enlightenment and therefore a godchild of Baruch Spinoza (a name conspicuously absent from this document). So I read this document as I would read any modern publication on the Bible, I assume the full panoply of post-Enlightenment understandings of the world in which we live. However much the post-modernist critiques (another notable absence in the Vatican document) of the Enlightenment may now be regarded as demanding a necessary rethinking of that axial event, I see no reason to imagine that post-modernism can reinscribe mediaevalism or a precritical approach to the Bible.

So, while I am very happy that the document has acknowledged the historical context out of which the Bible comes to us, I am not at all convinced that it has taken the full measure of what that means. Of the historical-critical approach to the Bible it seems to settle for the *historical* moiety of that description and to have downplayed the *critical* moiety. At least, I can find little serious critical reading of the Bible in the document, except in one or two sensitive areas. I gain from it no real sense of any awareness of the obscurity of parts of the Bible, of the difficulty of other parts, of the problems of translation and interpretation relating to an ancient alien book in ancient alien languages from ancient alien cultures, or of the fundamental cultural transformations required to understand or appropriate the book in the modern age. The Bible remains throughout this document as an absolute revelation from God, subject no doubt to ecclesiastical dogma and interpretation, but utterly unaffected by changes brought about by time, society or culture (except for the changes introduced for dogmatic reasons and reflecting the *sensus plenior* approach). Where such aspects of the human have affected the book in its original construction they may be subject to human scrutiny in terms of the best possible methods available, but the fundamental conviction remains of 'the Bible as word of God expressed in human language'. All of the human scholarship recommended in this document has as its ultimate purpose the clarification and explication of the Bible in such confessional terms. This is criticism in the service of the church and, while that is a perfectly proper thing for ecclesiastical people to be doing, it should not be confused with other more historical and contemporary ways of reading the Bible.

Such general observations apart, I should say that within the narrow constraints of its brief the document does provide an excellent account of a number of important aspects of current scholarship on the Bible. There is a good exposition of the historical-critical method, singling out the work of Richard Simon, Jean Astruc, Hermann Gunkel, Martin Dibelius and Rudolf Bultmann in particular. The value and limitations of the method are touched on and there is generally a positive attitude towards it. New methods of literary analysis are then examined and these include rhetorical analysis, narrative analysis, and semiotic analysis. Under the section on tradition-based approaches there is a focus on canonical criticism (Childs and Sanders), approaches using Jewish traditions of biblical interpretation, and the history of the influence of the text (*Wirkungsgeschichte*) approach. The human sciences contribution is the focus of the section of analysis on the sociological approach, the approach of cultural anthropology and approaches using psychological and psychoanalytical research. Here I detected the first strong note of dissent in the document:

> Whatever the circumstances, a psychology or psychoanalysis of an atheistic nature disqualifies itself from giving proper consideration to the data of faith. Useful as they may be to determine more

exactly the extent of human responsibility, psychology and psychoanalysis should not serve to eliminate the reality of sin and of salvation. (I.D.3, p. 37).

However, unless the document writers also assent to the proposition that theistic positions cannot give proper consideration to atheistic matters I cannot see the logic of this claim. It looks to me very much like another case of 'he who drives fat oxen must himself be fat' and sounds like authoritarian dogmatism favouring its own approaches and ruling out any approach considered to be threatening to its own interests. That is a political stance and it makes this document very much a political statement issued by the Vatican defining the boundaries of scholarly investigation beyond which it will permit no transgression.

Under contextual approaches there is a brief consideration of the liberationist approach and the feminist approach. Here again I detect dissent and a growing unease with some contemporary ways of reading the Bible. The practice of reading the Bible using 'an analysis inspired by materialist doctrines' is described as being a 'very questionable' practice, 'especially when it involves the Marxist principle of the class struggle' (I.E 2, p. 40). Of the many feminisms available for scrutiny, only three principal forms are isolated for comment: radical (denies all authority to the Bible), neo-orthodox (accepts Bible as prophetic and potentially of service), and critical (the rediscovery of women in the Bible). While accepting the positive aspects of some feminist positions, the document also is critical of the risk run by feminist exegesis 'of interpreting the biblical texts in a tendentious and thus debatable manner'. This tendency is regarded as being due to reading the Bible 'from a preconceived judgment'. As far as I am concerned (and I am no feminist!) this is just the pot calling the kettle black! If ever there was a tendentious reading of the Bible from a preconceived judgment position it is any and all ecclesiastical readings of the Bible in terms of the dogmas of *post-biblical* conciliar Christianity (what this document might call the *sensus plenior*). It is admitted that feminist exegesis can be useful, but 'only to the degree that it does not fall into the very traps it denounces' (true for every position I would have thought) and 'that it does not lose sight of the evangelical teaching concerning power as service, a teaching addressed by Jesus to all disciples, men and women'. Well, yes, I guess that is true. But 'power as service' can be a weasel phrase when used by the Vatican, and the history of the Christian churches in their dealings with women has been more marked by the imposition of power on them than of service to them. Men in the churches have had the power and women in the churches have done the service – not quite what the commands of Jesus appear to mean! While there come into my mind here echoes of a phrase from the Gospels about 'whited sepulchres', I have to admit that the 'question of women' may yet prove to be an Achilles heel of the Vatican.

At this point in the document there is yet another hiccup. The section on feminism ends with a footnote which I shall quote in full:

> Out of nineteen votes cast, the text of this last paragraph received eleven in favour, four against and there were four abstentions. Those who voted against it asked that the result of the vote be published along with the text. The commission consented to this.

Wow! I did not know that each paragraph was voted on and that all the other paragraphs in the document had been agreed unanimously. On the other hand, perhaps it was only this statement about 'power as service' which was contested and therefore voted on. And well it might be! I do not think that the Vatican is in any position to lecture the world on service, especially not women. In my judgment (I come from Catholic roots in Dublin, so speak from experience) 'power as service' – whatever that may mean – has been more displayed by Catholic women throughout Christian history than by most of those who would grant themselves the title 'servants of the servants of God'. Service certainly, but as to power I would have to canvass among the Catholic women of the world to find out whether they thought that their service to Mother Church was a form of power or otherwise. What I do find fascinating about this document are the points where the hiccups occur: psychology and psychoanalysis, atheistic thought, materialism and Marxism, and feminism. Modernity and the twentieth century still provide interlocutors the church would rather not engage with, except on its own terms. The old authoritarianism is still there, still entrenched and only the safe bits of contemporary biblical scholarship seem to be acceptable. This looks like scholarship as domestication of awkward issues and biblical scholarship as the smoothing out of difficulties encountered in the sacred text (the biblical scholar as skivvy!).

The final section in the methods and approaches for interpretation part of the document looks at fundamentalist interpretation of the Bible. The description is fair but mostly devoted to analysing the problems represented by fundamentalism. For fundamentalism is a diseased way of reading the Bible, so it inevitably warrants some consideration in any treatment of contemporary ways of reading the Bible. Fundamentalism 'actually invites people to a kind of intellectual suicide'. The critique here is sharp – as I would expect from the Vatican. Whatever criticisms may be directed against Vatican behaviour over the centuries, it can never be accused of fundamentalism. Unless we broaden that term to cover matters of dogma rather than limit it to describing attitudes towards and beliefs about the Bible, then the Catholic Church could only ever be accused of a tendency towards a dogmatics fundamentalism. On the Bible it is soundly non-fundamentalist. It makes an interesting political point in its criticism of fundamentalism as tending to adopt 'very narrow points of view':

> Its relying upon a non-critical reading of certain texts of the Bible serves to reinforce political ideas and social attitudes that are marked by prejudices – racism, for example – quite contrary to the Christian gospel.

Here (above on page 45) are the beginnings of a recognition of problems in the Bible, in the sense of translation problems and, as in the above citation, problems of a non-critical reading of certain texts. This is a very important and good point which I would have liked to have seen raised much earlier in the document. Perhaps the demand for *a critical reading of the Bible* has been implicit throughout the document, but I was not aware of it at all. Some things have to be said, openly and plainly, they can never be just assumed. An engagement with what constitutes a good, critical reading of the Bible would have made this a much more valuable document (in my opinion). As for racism being contrary to the gospel – I would like to see the steps in the argument for reading the Bible in relation to post-Enlightenment and contempoary social values such as good race relations. Racism not being an issue in biblical times, it is hard to see what the arguments might be. Now had the document said 'slavery' rather than 'racism', *that* would have been a most fascinating point of debate about a critical reading of the Bible because while the Bible may know nothing of racism it comes to us from a culture of slavery and knows slaves very well. In fact, after the Hebrew slaves were released from 'the house of bondage' in Egypt, the first set of laws given to them (after the decalogue) concerned the buying and selling of '*Hebrew* slaves'. So the slaves were freed from being slaves in order to be free to own slaves of their own (among other things)! Here I do wish the document had engaged with some real (cultural and moral) problems *in the Bible and the modern world* in order to demonstrate to the reader just how *a critical reading* of the Bible today might be fully carried out. Very much a missed opportunity in my judgment.

The point comes up again in the discussion towards the end of the document (IV. A.3, pp. 85f.) when 'limits' are discussed. All readings of the Bible are recognized as being selective, but 'tendentious interpretations' are readings which ought to be avoided. These are uses of the text for one's own 'narrow purposes' (as for example by Jehovah's Witnesses!) and include any actualization of the text 'at variance with the fundamental orientations of the biblical text as, for example, a rationalism which is opposed to faith or an atheistic materialism'. There, the magisterium has spoken again about transgressive modes of reading the Bible which will not be permitted! It goes on to say:

> Clearly to be rejected also is every attempt at actualization set in a direction contrary to evangelical justice and charity, such as, for example, the use of the Bible to justify racial segregation, anti-semitism or sexism whether on the part of men or of women. Particular attention is necessary, according to the spirit of the Second Vatican Council (*Nostra Aetate*, 4), to avoid absolutely any actualization of certain texts of the New Testament which could provoke or reinforce unfavourable attitudes to the Jewish people.

While I have no fundamental disagreement here with the sentiments expressed – they are admirable – I do not quite appreciate how one can know which bits of the Bible should be actualized in daily life and which bits should be avoided. I would like to have seen 'slavery' included in that list of bad things to be avoided (racism, anti-semitism, sexism) because there is so much slavery enforced throughout the Third World these days and slavery is very much a cultural element in the Bible (not spoken against by the evangelical justice and charity of the New Testament either!). But the point about anti-semitism does raise the issue most acutely and I applaud the document when it instructs the reader 'to avoid absolutely any actualization of certain texts of the New Testament'. That phrase 'certain texts of the New Testament' is one of the glories of this document for me. I find it profoundly evocative and encouraging as a warning against taking everything in the Bible seriously. One of the many moments of glory of Vatican II was its renunciation of the ancient charge of 'deicide' against the Jews. Yet the anti-semitic texts of the New Testament are there and must be avoided. How? Just how do we know which are the 'certain texts' to be avoided?

The document explains the 'how' in traditionalist terms:

> False paths will be avoided if actualization of the biblical message begins with a correct interpretation of the text and continues within the stream of the living tradition, under the guidance of the church's magisterium.

So what's new? Apart from the question-begging 'correct interpretation of the text', the magisterium is the answer. That is fine (up to a point) for Catholics, but what does it have to do with contemporary biblical scholarship? The historical-critical method is at best only aligned to the magisterium when its findings fit in with dogmatic theology and therefore it loses its critical edge. The critique of the magisterium which is so much at the heart of Protestantism makes this document look so much less radical than it may appear at first sight to many non-Catholic readers. I readily accept that that is no problem for the Vatican or for some Catholic readers, but it does mean that once again the clothes may be those of Esau but the voice

is most definitely that of Jacob. The old *casta meretrix* is still
pursuing her ancient calling, I fear!

But the really important point for me has little to do with
magisterial judgments. The magisterium is a matter for Catholics
to quarrel about. What interests me here is the principle that
'certain texts' of the Bible are such that they must in no way be
actualized in the life of the reader or the church. I think that
principle is worth a thousand magisterial proclamations and it is for
me the most important signal in this document. What I would
dearly love to have seen would have been the arguments justifying
the principle. What drives the 'correct interpretation' here? If it is
the magisterium, then what drives its thinking here? While theological rhetoric may refer to 'God' or 'the Holy Spirit', that is not a
very perceptive explanation – it does not explain why either 'being'
failed for centuries to educate the magisterium in values which the
Enlightenment was able to generate quite quickly. For me, the
abandonment of the text at such vital points reflects post-Enlightenment thinking reading the Bible while clinging to as much of it as
still remains possible by way of resisting the 'acids of modernity'.
Some of the philosophies despised or denounced by the document
have, over recent centuries, helped to humanize Christianity and I
think proper recognition of 'the Other' (that is, all those atheistic or
secular systems outside the churches) is long overdue. I wish the
Vatican document had reflected further on 'the limits' to applying
the Bible to life today, because therein are to be found some
important features of the post-Enlightenment development of
critical biblical studies.

The document is too rich and varied (as befits any document on
the Bible) for me to be able to respond adequately to all its sections.
I have mostly ignored Chapters II and III on 'Hermeneutical Questions' and 'Characteristics of Catholic Interpretation' in order to
focus on Chapters I and IV. The material on *relectures*, among so
many fine things, caught my eye, as did the discussions on *lectio
divina* and liturgy, but space is not available for a full set of critical
reflections on the whole document. I want to conclude with
considering one other aspect of the document which engaged my
attention. It bears on the discussion above about which and what
texts should be used today and how we might know what ones to

avoid. Most of the advocacies in the document I shall leave aside, but one commands my scrutiny. In the section on moral theology and exegesis and in the section on the pastoral ministry the same point is made: 'On the most important points the moral principles of the Decalogue remain basic.' (p. 80) and 'catechesis . . . will single out the Decalogue' (p. 91). That singling out of the decalogue is an ancient Christian practice and one reinscribed in the English churches after the Reformation (after the stripping of the altars, boards with the decalogue written on them often were placed above or about the communion table). Now, there are lots of problems with the decalogue in the Bible, so this singling out of one specific biblical *pericope* should not be imagined to be any easy solution to the question of which bits of the Bible should be read and internalized and which bits (those 'certain texts') should be avoided.

Among the fundamental problems of understanding the decalogue, once you have got past the problems of which text, which reading and which numbering system should be used and have decided that the New Testament reduction of it to one or two love commands does not transform it adequately into a Christian ethic of relationship, are the problems of interpreting its commands and determining what the modern cultural equivalents of them might be. It is all very well blandly regarding them as 'the moral law'. The Bible knows nothing of such matters. Nor does it know anything about the decalogue as a set of universals. On the contrary, these statements are a structural part of the covenant between YHWH and Israel and to transfer them *simpliciter* to the Christian churches is to interfere with scripture without any good warrant. In order to use the decalogue various churches have had to reinterpret its terms radically and apply them in ways unimaginable to the biblical writers. However, let's just concentrate on meaning in the text and ignore the history of the text's interpretation. What does it mean to say 'thou shalt not kill'? Well, if a modern pacifist is reading the command it will mean many things, whereas if a modern mercenary is reading it it will mean many things less! Who will decide what it means? Will the historical-critical biblical scholars be allowed to apply their scientific exegetical methods to discovering the historical meaning of such inculturated words? Reading the Bible through as a means of understanding the far from simple command 'do not kill' seems to rule out reading the ancient Israelis as being pacifistic, vegetarian, cloth-wearing quietists. For the command does not appear to have been understood in those times as ruling out killing animals for sacrifice to YHWH or as food to eat for oneself. Nor does the command seem to have legislated against war, slaughter or capital punishment. Indeed, by the time the whole Hebrew Bible has been read through for warrants backing a historical interpretation of the ruling the commandment seems only to rule out unsocial killing between people not authorized to kill anybody. Do not unnecessarily kill people who should not be killed unnecessarily. A bit tautological perhaps, but that seems to be a fair meaning of the text *in its historical context*. While I cannot imagine anybody disagreeing with that, nor can I imagine anybody regarding it as being capable of being universalized as a *moral* rule. That transformation seems to belong to the departure from treating the Bible as a historical cultural production and to the imposition on the Bible of a dogma of revelation and moral law. I understand the *Rezeptionsgeschichte* of the text whereby with time and through many cultural transformations it came to be read otherwise, but I would insist on regarding such developments as being extra-textual and I would not reinscribe the text according to such subsequent transformations. This may well be a real limitation of the historical-critical approach to reading the Bible, but every approach has severe limits.

For the magisterium the *sensus plenior* approach to interpreting the Bible may help to overcome the limitations of the historical meaning of the text. But the *Rezeptionsgeschichte* of the Bible has produced an enormous amount of material reflecting the multitudinous ways the Bible can be and has been interpreted. For me such a complex and complicated history of reading the Bible prompts the question 'once the historical meaning gives way to subsequent meanings, why limit interpretation to specific moments in the past?' The Bible does not stop being interpreted after the period of the church councils. So when it comes to the decalogue why not incorporate the whole history of its interpretation into any account of its meaning? Hence the epigraphic preface to these critical reflections comes from William Blake's famous treatment of the decalogue. As usual and as befits a great reader of the Bible Blake works well the fundamental shift in consciousness between the time of the Jewish Bible and Jesus. I have to say that I think Blake's reading of the decalogue is a better *Christian* reading of the text than the magisterium's treatment of it as 'the moral law'. But for all those Catholics who still recognize the authority of the Vatican it will be sufficient for the magisterium to arbitrate between meanings of scripture.

We did not, however, need this document to tell us that the magisterium determines meaning in the Bible, whatever biblical scholarship may say. We have always known that! So what *is* new about this document? Perhaps it is only the discourse used in it which is new. The welcome given to so many different contemporary ways of reading the Bible is certainly good to see. Permission to use modern scholarship probably does need to be spelled out for the faithful. But in a real sense nothing has changed. The magisterium is still there. It is still in control. It is still governing how the Bible is to be read and it is still dictating what is important and what is not important (the identity of the preface writer is the sign under which the inscribed document should be read — let the reader understand!). There may well be greater openness to different methods of studying the Bible. That is certainly true and welcome it is. But the document is still about authority, control and the application of dogmatics to the Bible. Any method which helps to reinforce the Christian understanding of the Bible is praised, whereas any method which raises awkward problems or which is suspected of having roots in alien philosophies is ruled out of order. The document is wonderfully modern on the surface, but it is woefully old-fashioned and magisterial in its depths. Now that is what I would expect from any document issued by today's deeply reactionary Vatican. The document never quite escapes from its Vatican atmosphere of authority and control.

In the final analysis I would have to say: perhaps the clothes do belong to Esau, but listen to the voice. Whose voice do you hear in this document? What do you hear? How do you hear? Now go read the document again, reread (*relecture*) it better, but listen carefully to the voice in this document. How readest thou? Still a question well worth asking. Yet this also is a document worth reading and worth pondering long and hard. But let the reader understand. The study of the Bible may well be the soul of theology, but such a soul has many cracks in it. Cracks which no amount of documents like this very fine one from the Vatican can ever hope to paper over.

7

A Liturgist's Response

Kenneth Stevenson

> The treasures of the Bible are to be opened up more lavishly so that a
> richer fare may be provided for the faithful at the table of God's word.
> In this way a more representative part of the sacred scriptures will be
> read to the people in the course of a prescribed number of years.[1]

This oft-quoted recommendation from the Second Vatican
Council's Constitution on the Sacred Liturgy is full of promise, and
even with the hindsight of more than thirty years, it is hard to imagine
the excitement that lies between its lines, or the radical shift in
Roman Catholic life that it heralded. I can remember attending
masses in France during summer-holidays from the late 1950s
through to the late 1960s, in the course of which it was not difficult to
chart the growing use of the vernacular for the old lections, followed
by experimental use of the new scheme. The point of departure was
High Mass in Chartres Cathedral on an August Sunday morning in
1958, at which the preacher sent the verger firmly back to the sacristy
to fetch a book with the Gospels in French, a fitting prelude to a
homily I can recall on the pharisee and the publican. The point of
arrival was High Mass in Brussels Cathedral on 15 August 1968,
when the Old Testament lesson took its place alongside Epistle and
Gospel.

The change in reading-scheme is far more radical than even the
chronicle I have just outlined. For the readings at mass which the
Roman Catholic Church used until the recent changes were part of a
scheme that went back to the early Middle Ages. There was always
variation, but the basic core of these lections probably dates from
Carolingian times, and the festal and solemn-season passages are
even earlier. In his book on the liturgical reforms after the Second

Vatican Council, Annibale Bugnini recounts with what care his church entered upon the new project. Ecumenical feelers were extended in order to ascertain what the Church of England and the various Lutheran and Reformed churches were doing in the way of change.[2] I am even told that there were those on the Consilium Liturgicum who were against altering the old scheme – not because they were against change! – but because they felt it important that separated churches should at least use the same scripture-passages at their main Sunday services. This indeed was the case, in the main, for the Anglican Prayer Book and classical Lutheran books had kept the mediaeval readings on the whole intact. But new winds were blowing and they proved irresistible.

The old lectionary had developed along a basically synthetic line. Priority was usually given to the Gospel of Matthew, traditionally regarded as the earliest, in the 'bread-and-butter' readings at mass. John was the favoured festal and solemn-season evangelist; hence John 1.1–14 at Christmas, John 2.1–11 after Epiphany, the John passion narrative on Good Friday, John 20.1–10 on Easter morning, and John 14.15–30 at Pentecost. This is not to say that Mark and Luke do not appear – far from it. Indeed, one can see Luke's historical framework shaping the liturgical year and calendar, with Ascension, and the festivals of John the Baptist and the Virgin Mary. Once upon a time, some of these Gospel passages were read with Old Testament lections, but the Old Testament started to fall out of use in the West at the eucharist, probably from about the fifth century, though it persisted at, for example, Milan.

If one compares the old scheme with the principle enunciated at Vatican II that 'the treasures of the Bible are to be opened . . .', it does not take much imagination to realize that a new lectionary was inevitable. The work of liturgical drafting after the Council was handed over to various study groups, made up of experts. It is interesting to see from Bugnini's account that the initial task was to look at all the lectionaries extant (from Syriac through to the Old Testament scheme used in the 1960 Prayer Book of the Church of India, Pakistan, Burma and Ceylon).[3] Having done this spadework, it became clear to them that the mediaeval scheme had so many weaknesses and omissions that an entirely new lectionary was needed. So the next stage was reached, in which biblical scholars were called in to look at each one of the books of the Bible to see how they could be employed in the celebration of the eucharist. The list of names is as distinguished as the liturgists who carried out the archaeology on the old lectionaries. Thus, Cazelles was responsible for examining Leviticus, Numbers and Deuteronomy, whereas Schnackenburg studied the Corinthian epistles and those to Timothy. During this process, agreement emerged that this new lectionary should be an entirely new departure, based on a three-year Sunday cycle, and a two-year cycle for week-days.

It is not clear who took this strategic decision. What is clear is that the liturgists and biblical scholars were working in co-operation, which is a matter of significance in itself. The main shape of the Sunday lectionary is well known. The three years are devoted to each one of the Synoptics in turn, John taking prominence every year at the festal and solemn-season occasions, and also filling in the (slender) Marcan year. Epistle-material is read in course, chosen to fit in with the season, with Acts dominating the Easter provision. The Old Testament lections fitted easily into the high occasions, but the typological approach in what is called 'ordinary time' is the main target of criticism in the process of producing an ecumenical version of this lectionary, which culminated in the recent 'Revised Common Lectionary'.[4] This explains why Revised Common Lectionary has produced an alternative Old Testament scheme in 'ordinary time', which instead reads selected material in a serial fashion.

I have gone into some detail about the 1969 Lectionary, and its main, ecumenical offspring, because of its intrinsic importance (it is likely to become the main, international lectionary of churches in the mainstream 'liturgical' traditions worldwide); but also because it raises in itself principles of lectionary production at a time when biblical criticism and interpretation had been able to exert influences on the way modern lectionaries are compiled in a way that has not been the case before. For example, if one looks at the other main lectionary-scheme in use in the British Isles today, the 1967 Joint Liturgical Group two-year cycle,[5] it is not hard to discern behind its pages a desire to harmonize books of the Bible into a coherent whole, which owes a great debt to the 'biblical theology' movement that was in the ascendant in the 1950s. Liturgists do listen to biblical scholars! But biblical scholars do not speak with a single voice –

hence the importance of the Vatican document, with its careful enunciation of the very differing kinds of biblical criticism and interpretation. But if one compares the three-year lectionary, with its course-reading in Epistles and Gospels, and its concentration on one particular Gospel for each of the three years, it is even less hard to discern behind its pages a whiff of redaction- and traditio-historical criticism. This is strengthened even further if the alternative tracks of Old Testament readings in the Revised Common Lectionary are added to the picture. What this alternative seems to be saying is, if you don't want a typological approach to the Old Testament, then there is the narrative approach to individual authors. The strength of the three-year lectionary could be even further highlighted by the recent emphasis in canonical criticism on reading whole chunks of narrative, in order to supply as full a context as possible. On the other hand, the tendency to cut down narratives, particularly in the Old Testament, in order to make them manageable at Sunday eucharists, could be said to do damage to this very principle.

There is, of course, no such thing as the perfect lectionary. Whether one is dealing with a conservative set of one-year Sunday Epistles and Gospels (as in the pre-1969 Roman scheme, so influential, too, on Anglican and Lutheran practice until recent changes), or with the elaborate three-year Sunday scheme of three eucharistic readings, there is bound to be compromise of principles, if only in a few places (at best!), simply in order to complete the provision at all.

But biblical criticism is not only a tool for the scholar and the student. The Vatican document rightly emphasizes the principle of 'actualization', in line with the Constitution on the Sacred Liturgy's own tenor and overall thrust. This means, positively, that scripture is – in some sense – allowed to 'speak for itself', as a symbolic action, a feeding of the imagination, a nourishing of the soul. In this respect, the second part of the Vatican document is an eloquent counterblast to those who regard biblical scholarship as merely cerebral. Its general hostility to fundamentalism is refreshing, and it can be said without too much difficulty that churches which use a lectionary, of whatever kind, are less likely to inculcate a creeping fundamentalism, precisely because 'the treasures of the Bible are . . . opened up more lavishly' to congregations as they worship.

Biblical criticism also has an important 'critical' function in relation to reading the scriptures in worship. There is the obvious role of informing the preacher – and this is an ever-crying need – of the real complexities of the passages in question. It never ceases to amaze me that gifted preachers so easily avoid challenging questions in their sermons to congregations who are getting tired of being treated like spiritual infants. Even those well-attended 'Family Services' have many people present who are not going to leave their minds outside the church door just because this way of worshipping may be new or unfamiliar.

We noted earlier how canonical criticism may object to narratives being abbreviated in order to facilitate concentration and reading. There is always going to be conflict between the liturgist, who tends to live with a normative approach to the length of a lection in church (apart from solemn and special occasions, like Good Friday's passion narrative) and the ideology of a particular school of biblical studies. History shows that the liturgist tends to win, either because liturgists tend to be more conservative in this area or because they are sensitive to consumer-demand.

There are instances where motivations for change provide a fascinating back-drop to the liturgical-biblical scene. One is to be seen in the Gospel narrative for 2 February, the feast of Candlemas or the Presentation of Christ in the Temple. As I have shown in a recent study,[6] the universal practice in the East is to read the whole narrative, from Luke 2.22–40, with the appearance of Joseph, Mary and Jesus in the temple and the prophecies of Simeon as well as Anna. But things have not been so simple in the West. The normal practice was to confine the reading to Simeon's oracle, and stop at the end of what is called the Nunc Dimittis (Luke 2.32). This canticle, now chiefly associated with Evensong, was in the Middle Ages sung before mass on this feast during the distribution of the candles; it was only latterly absorbed into the office of Compline (whence it made its entry into Anglican Evensong).[7] It could be said that to conclude the Gospel for the day with that canticle made its own point. However, in 1549, the Gospel was abbreviated further, stopping at the point where Simeon appears (Luke 2.27a); and there it stayed until 1662, when (probably thanks to John Cosin's knowledge of Eastern customs), Anna's part in the drama was added, so that the reading ended at Luke 2.40. As if to make matters even more complex, the Alternative Service Book (1980) has, in effect, two celebrations of the feast: the Sunday After Christmas (Year 2), when the Gospel is the longer one (Luke 2.22–40), and on 2 February, when it is a shorter version (Luke 2.22–35 – which includes Simeon's second oracle, but still leaves out Anna). The 1991 *Promise of His Glory* gives the longer version, without the option to shorten.

Other such case-studies could doubtless be made and it can be hazardous to speculate on the motivations for fresh composition (the initial introduction of a festival or observance) and change (adapting the tradition). But the factors at work in this particular instance are not hard to see. The East, with its egalitarian marriage rites, in which both partners are crowned, is also even-handed in its perception of what this feast is about, a trait, moreover, expressed in the traditional iconography, where Anna nearly always appears. The West, with its less egalitarian marriage-rite, in which the bride is veiled and only she is blessed at the nuptial benediction, excludes Anna from the Candlemas scene. The Anglican Prayer Book initially takes this trend further, goes right back on it, and then more recently reverts to exclusion, until rescued. Interestingly, the 1969 Roman Lectionary gives the whole pericope, but permits the shorter version. Here is a classic case where the combination of feminist criticism, with a touch of canonical interpretation, has been a motivation for change, or at least supplies the groundwork for a fuller approach to the tradition – here represented by the (seldom-changing) Christian East.[8]

The relationship between Bible and Liturgy is never going to be entirely straightforward. In a paper read to the Societas Liturgica at its 1991 meeting in Toronto, Paul Bradshaw, in an historical overview, points to what he calls 'the essentially multivalent nature of the use to which scripture has been put in Christian worship',[9] in which he goes beyond lections to include such subtle features as the influence of scripture on the writing of prayer-texts. However, this is not intended as an excuse for saying that anything goes. Rather, it is a warning against the hasty production of lectionaries that are 'politically correct' in relation to what may turn out to be passing fads. In this respect, the two-year Joint Liturgical Group 'thematic' approach has clearly dated, whereas the three-year Roman Catholic cycle continues to stand the test of time, though it will have to heed specific points of criticism as these mount up over the years. These are more likely to be effective as liturgical usage is fed by combinations of different kinds of biblical interpretation. Here, the Western wobbliness over Candlemas is a case in point. But there will be many other such examples. Moreover, readings that assume a difficult allegorical interpretation, e.g. Gal. 4.21ff., the old epistle for the Fourth Sunday in Lent, have been avoided in the new lectionaries. The overall impression that the Vatican document provides is, however, that the dialogue and the critique should continue. For obvious reasons, it has not been possible here to look into a whole host of other issues, including the rationale of the ultra-short 'chapter' readings from scripture in the Roman Catholic Liturgy of the Hours (in some ways comparable to the often unsatisfactory sentences peppered through the *ASB*), or the way in which scripture feeds (directly or by suggestion) prayer writing and also hymn composition. Meanwhile, the Vatican has done the whole Church Catholic a service, not only in producing the best (though hardly faultless) modern lectionary to date, but also – a quarter of a century on – a clear, judicious, and comprehensive tool for the evaluation of the use of the Bible by Christians, in worship, study, and meditation.

Notes

1 Austin Flannery OP (ed.), *Vatican Council II: The Conciliar and Post-Conciliar Documents*, Collegeville: Liturgical Press 1980, p. 17 (art. 51). See ibid., p. 171, General Instruction on the Roman Missal, art. 34, 'In the readings, the table of God's word is laid before the people and the treasures of the Bible are opened.'

2 Annibale Bugnini, *La Riforma liturgica (1948–1975)*, (Bibliotheca Ephemerides Liturgicae Subsidia 30), Rome: Edizioni Liturgiche 1983, pp. 401ff.

3 *The Book of Common Prayer . . . According to the use of the Church of India, Pakistan, Burma and Ceylon*, Madras, Delhi, Lahore: ISPCK 1960.

4 See *Ordo Lectionum Missae* (editio typica), Typis Polyglottis Vaticanis 1969. Compare with *The Revised Common Lectionary: The Consultation on Common Texts*, Canterbury Press 1992. Some of the proposals and variations in the latter were published in an interim version, for experimental use and

evaluation, in *Common Lectionary: The Lectionary Proposed by the Consultation on Common Texts*, New York: Church Hymnal Corporation n.d.

5 See Ronald C. D. Jasper, *The Calendar and Lectionary: A Reconsideration*, Oxford University Press 1967. This formed the basis of the lection-schemes produced by the ensuing service-books of Anglican, Methodist, Prebyterian, Baptist, and United Reformed Churches.

6 See Kenneth Stevenson, 'The Ceremonies of Light – Their Shape and Function in the Paschal Vigil Liturgy', *Ephemerides Liturgicae* 99 (1985), pp. 170–185.

7 See F. E. Brightman, *The English Rite II*, Rivingtons 1915, pp. 566–569. Monastic compline has proved resistant to outside influence: the monks of Quarr Abbey, on the Isle of Wight, part of the Solesmes Congregation of Benedictines, have only recently allowed the Nunc Dimittis to be sung at Compline.

8 See *Making Women Visible: The Use of Inclusive Language with the ASB* (A Report by the Liturgical Commission of the General Synod of the Church of England), Church House Publishing 1988, p. 63, for a table of lections in which women figure prominently, and which do not appear in the ASB 1980 lectionary. (Many of these do not appear in the 1969 Sunday 3-year lectionary, or its ecumenical equivalents, either.)

9 See Paul Bradshaw, 'The Use of the Bible in Liturgy: Some Historical Perspectives', *Studia Liturgica* 22 (1992), pp. 35–52.

Contributors

Paul M. Blowers is Associate Professor of Church History at Emmanuel School of Religion in Johnson City, Tennessee

Robert P. Carroll is Professor of Old Testament Studies in the University of Glasgow

Peter Hebblethwaite was a freelance writer on Roman Catholic affairs and the author of *Pope Paul VI: The First Modern Pope* (1993) and *The Next Pope* (1995)

Jan Holman is Professor in the Theological Faculty of the University of Tilburg in the Netherlands

Leslie Houlden is Emeritus Professor of Theology at King's College, London

John D. Levenson is the Albert A. List Professor of Jewish Studies at Harvard University

John Muddiman is University Lecturer in New Testament Studies and Fellow of Mansfield College in the University of Oxford

Kenneth Stevenson is Rector of Holy Trinity Church, Guildford and a member of the Liturgical Commission of the Church of England

Robert L. Wilken is the William R. Kenan Jr Professor of the History of Christianity at the University of Virginia

For Further Reading

John Barton, *People of the Book?*, SPCK and Westminster/John Knox 1988

J. T. Burtchaell, *Catholic Theories of Biblical Inspiration since 1810*, Cambridge University Press 1969

Robert Carroll, *Wolf in the Sheepfold*, SPCK 1991 and Trinity Press International 1991 with the title *The Bible as a Problem for Theology*

R. J. Coggins and J. L. Houlden (eds), *A Dictionary of Biblical Interpretation*, SCM Press and Trinity Press International 1990

Raymond F. Collins, *Introduction to the New Testament*, Doubleday and SCM Press 1992

J. L. Houlden, *Bible and Belief*, SPCK 1991

J. L. Houlden, *Connections*, SCM Press 1986

Stephen Neill and Tom Wright, *The Interpretation of the Bible 1861–1986*, Oxford University Press 1988

J. Rogerson, C. Rowland and B. Lindars, *The Study and Use of the Bible*, Marshall Pickering and Eerdmans 1988

G. N. Stanton, *The Gospels and Jesus*, Oxford University Press 1989

Christopher Tuckett, *Reading the New Testament*, SPCK 1987

Alec R. Vidler, *The Modernist Movement in the Roman Catholic Church*, Cambridge University Press 1934

Francis B. Watson (ed.) *The Open Text*, SCM Press 1993

Francis B. Watson, *Text, Church and World: Biblical Interpretation in Theological Perspective*, T. & T. Clark and Eerdmans 1994

University of Chester